ENRICO ROLLA

Like it or Leave it

The adventure begins within

Written by: Enrico Rolla (www.iwatson.com; www.iwatsoneducation.com)
Cover: Cristina Cecconato – acapoagency, Torino (design and graphics)
Layout: Cristina Cecconato – acapoagency, Torino
Translation: Elaine Wright
Editing: Istituto Watson Edizioni
C.so Vinzaglio 12/bis, Torino, Italy
Tel. + 39 011 5611102 fax + 39 011 5611102
e-mail: info@iwatson.com – progetti@iwatson.com
www.iwatson.com
www.iwatsoneducation.com

Printed by:
CreateSpace
CreateSpeace Indipendent Publishing Platform
www.createspace.com

First Edition: 1987 Torino
© by SEI-Società Editrice Internazionale (20 reprints)

First Edition English: 2017
© Istituto Watson Edizioni
C.so Vinzaglio 12/bis,
Torino10121, Italy

Contents

Foreward

The first edition of this book was published in Italian in 1987. It deals with behaviour modification through assertiveness, expectation management and awareness-raising.

'Like it or Leave it' continues successfully to sell today in Italy and was one of the reasons for which, thirty years on, I decided to publish it in English.

The content is as relevant and valid today as it was when it was written, so I have not made any changes to the book.

Motivation to write came from observation of the world around us; ever more competitive and stressful in environments in which we are forced to fight if we want to emerge and in the increasingly difficult relationships with friends and family. Often the burden is too heavy and in time it affects our persona, our true being.

Over the years I have trained individuals and companies on assertiveness, on the management of their feelings, on how to learn self-motivation and above all, on how to make use of a particular thought process which I call irony.

I have also seen many so-called motivational courses flourishing, promising to change people's lives in two or three days and many books pitching slogans such as 'How to Be Happy in 10 Moves' or '5 Steps to Conquer the World', as if our inner well-being could be acquired by applying a set of rules. I have always believed this to be wrong and if the need is to read a self-help book, we should not expect some easy rule of thumb to follow, like a cooking recipe. Better instead, points to ponder help acquire the necessary skills to grow and reach goals.

In this book I tell the story of how difficult it is to gain approval be it from friends, family or colleagues when we have low self-belief and are unsure of our own worth. Examples and dialogues taken from everyday life become the pretext to better understand the dynamics of many behaviors that make us feel bad, so we can change, and start feeling good.

The book's focus is development of the word "self-esteem", meaning the opinion we have about ourselves, the image of ourselves that we have built over time, starting from the family environment, and formed day after day by our life experiences.

'Like it or Leave it' essentially talks about this, because everyone, at some point, has felt inadequate or afraid of other's opinion and if we are assertive we can accept it. Being assertive does not mean being violent towards others, nor does it mean putting up with others behaviour. It means accepting their point of view and defending your own, and clearly and effectively express feelings and opinions without offending or attacking.

My intention is not to dispense pearls of wisdom and life tips, rather, I hope to encourage self-reflection to help you look at life from a different perspective and manage interpersonal relationships with greater balance.

My hope is that in reading this book will bring the mindfulness that all of us, as individuals, can, and will aspire to changing perspective to learn to live better with ourselves and others.

The applied method is based on Cognitive Behaviour Therapy, recognised world over as elective treatment for treating panic attacks and wich efficiency and results are scientifically proven. Over 80% of people undergoing therapy have obtained a positive short-term outcome and long-term reduction of relapse.

Introduction

We have all been submissive or aggressive at some point in a given situation, left wondering if we could have behaved differently.

It is not always easy to know how to behave in every circumstance. A lack of social skills and difficulty in managing interpersonal relationships tend to generate social anxiety. Many of us are uncomfortable in accepting criticism or communicating our mood or feelings. These and other situations create a heightened state of tension and awkwardness, leading us to witndrawal from or avoidance of such situations. The aim of Assertive Training is to learn appropriate behaviour. The question is: What sort of behaviour can be considered appropriate?

Neither passivity nor aggressiveness is appropriate; both will generate a sense of frustration or discomfort. It is thus essential to learn new behaviour so we neither put up with, nor are aggressive towards others. We define 'assertive' as a more acceptable and balanced behaviour.

Examples of assertive behaviour include making or refusing requests, accepting other people's opinions, starting a conversation or sustaining a different point of view.

Assertive Training is widely used in cognitive behavioural therapy. Its development and spread derives from evidence that 70% of the population tends to be afflicted with social or rapport-related anxiety. Andrew Salter (1949) is considered precursor to Assertive Training, Joseph Wolpe (1969) later introduced the idea in cognitive behavioural therapy.

Behavioural therapy is a combination of experimentation and technologies developed on the basis of experimental psychological research on learning.

Theory and experimentation from Pavlov to the more recent results of Skinner, Miller, Bandura and Eysenck have identified the basic laws by which humans learn, gather ideas and behaviours. Thereafter, operational guidelines were provided to trace back to the cause or reason of any given behaviour and consequently extinguish, modify or establish a more adequate performance.

Methodological accuracy and scientific rigor in treatment analysis and control of results are the main characteristics of behavioural therapy.

This experimental method applied to individual cases, as regards both clinical investigation and therapy has given the percentages of success obtained in the specific areas:

— Single symptom phobias (such as fear of animals, fear of heights) 95%.
— Phobias (e.g. agoraphobia, fear of pain) 85%.
— Obsessions and depression 70%.
— Social anxiety 70%.

— Obesity 20%.

— Alcoholism 5-10%.

The percentage of success, in all cases treated, are for follow up carried out at one year and three years from the end of treatment. Average treatment duration was twenty sessions.

When the patient requests help to learn how to manage anxiety-producing interpersonal situations, a behavioural psychologist will customarily use two procedures:

1) Behaviour repetition.
2) Simulation.

In behaviour repetition the therapist reproduces and mimes the anxiety producing behaviour, while the patient plays himself. Then, having identified the verbal and non-verbal cues that the patient needs to change, they move through to the next step-simulation. During this phase, the therapist plays the part of the patient and demonstrates a preferable behaviour type for the various situations; for example, by demonstrating how to address criticism, make requests or express views without feeling anxiety. Obviously, these skills learned in the therapy room must be used and practiced in everyday life.

Often, in practice, it is difficult to transfer these skills from the therapy room to real life. We may rationally believe it is inappropriate to attack or suffer others and we may have mastered some communication skills, but once *that* particular adverse situation arises we tend to issue our habitual and 'erroneous' behaviour, for example:

— Criticism at work: We keep feelings in in check momentarily but shortly after lose control and become aggressive.

— Disagreements at work: Initially we handle it, but soon calm gives way to feelings of tension and anger.

If we are feeling resentful, how can we be assertive? If we are envious of someone else's achievements, how can we, in their presence, remain cool, calm and comfortable?

Feeling resentment or envy for someone begins with an erroneous thinking pattern, or from maintaining rigid suppositions that do not allow behaviour change.

This book considers two relentlessly interacting behaviour patterns:

1) Verbal and non-verbal behaviour, that is, the skills required to facilitate interpersonal communication;
2) Cognitive behaviour, that is, the 'baggage' of thoughts or suppositions that can have a significant effect on interpersonal relationships.

A 'failure' in interpersonal relationships can activate negative, disturbing thoughts, and negative and disturbing thoughts can be detrimental to our future performance.

Behaviour Styles

Assertive Behaviour

A friend asks a favour which we really should turn down, but we end up complying.

We receive a compliment but it makes us feel uncomfortable and don't know how to respond.

We are brought bad wine at the restaurant and don't know how to make a complaint.

An acquaintance says something we do not agree with; we would like to express our point of view, but remain silent.

Someone senior criticizes our work, we'd like to seek further clarification, but do nothing.

Suffering others, unable to express ourselves, having difficulty making decisions, thinking that others are better, afraid of judgment and asking for approval, being unable to say no, indicates a passive style of behaviour. Often a passive person will issue aggressive behaviour, feel guilty, but later return to the usual, passive behaviour. Suffering these situations leads to a heightened sense of frustration; we feel helpless and tend to isolate or withdraw.

Our speech patterns are typical, 'You are absolutely incapable', 'I was expecting much more from you', 'If you really were a friend you would behave differently', 'I'm telling you for your own good because I care about you', 'I know it is right to tell you this', 'Work is not going well because my staff are hopeless'. Violating others' rights in the utter conviction that we never make mistakes, the belief that those mistakes belong to somebody else, being unaccepting of other people's point of view, over-estimation of self, hyper-evaluation, refusing to be swayed even when evidence of the mistake points to us, blaming, putting down and presuming the right to judge, are all typical behaviours of the aggressive personality.

Assertiveness sits between aggressive and passive. It is neither violating others nor allowing or putting up with aggressiveness. In being assertive we accept different points of view, we are ready to change opinion, we believe others do not behave just to please, we show respect and are not possessive or judgmental.

Using the subject 'I' is assertive behaviour. 'You', on the other hand, is aggressive. We can say 'I do not like', 'I do not want', 'I am uncomfortable'. This is the correct way to communicate our feelings. It is aggressive to say: 'You are upsetting me'. 'You do not understand me'. We are delegating our discomfort, when in fact, the discomfort is our own.

You are probably asking if the assertive personality really exists. I'm sure you must know the feeling of being able to talk freely to someone without feeling criticised or put down. If you have experienced such a situation, then you can safely presume that this type of person does exist.

The distinction between the various types of behaviour (passive, aggressive, assertive) is mostly theoretical. Often we slip between one behaviour type and the other. We can be assertive in one situation and yet aggressive in another. An individual can be assertive at work, having learned that being aggressive is a disadvantageous consequence. But, that same person, on returning home, may show aggressive behaviour towards his family. Another person at work may be passive, but assume aggressive behaviour at home. Behaviour indeed, tends to be situational.

Manipulative Strategies

There are basically three types of manipulative behaviours. We have probably manifested all three at some time or another. They are:

1) Blaming
2) Inferiorization /putting down
3) Erratic behaviour

An adult daughter comes home after eating out at a time the mother considers too late. On entering the mother retorts, 'If you're not home at a reasonable time I can't get to sleep and you worry me to death.'

A father wants his married son to visit more often, when his son calls, his father barks, 'Do you realize a whole week has gone by and you haven't called, I might be sick and you just don't care'.

A friend asks a favour, on refusal of which he replies: 'I didn't expect *you* to turn me down. You've always been able to count on me, and I thought you were a friend.'

These are just a few examples of frequently used guilt-inducing clichés.

So what do we hope to obtain using this behaviour?

1. *That our discomfort diminishes.* This may be the case of the mother worried about the daughter's late arrival. We see the following scheme:

a) Daughter is out, mother is worried and ill at ease.
b) She attributes her discomfort to the daughter's behaviour.
c) She blames the daughter by saying 'you worry me to death'.
d) While the daughter is out she too feels discomfort, thinking about her mother waiting for her to return. She frequently checks the time and her discomfort increases.
e) She reduces her discomfort by arriving on time.
f) In doing so she will be considered 'a good girl'.

2. *That we get what we want.* This is when we don't want a friend to reject our request for a favour. In this situation those who use the guilt-inducing technique are not necessarily feeling discomfort. They do it to get what they want. The friend, feeling guilty, gives in to the request.

If we are blamed we may feel or do the following:

a) Huge discomfort, which we try to reduce by simply enduring the situation. This is followed by a sense of frustration and powerlessness and is tightly connected to low self-esteem.
b) Experience some discomfort, but know how to manage this

type of manipulation. If guilty feelings then ensue, it is likely that there will be a return to passive behaviour.

c) Experience discomfort and become aggressive with those they are blaming. This breaks rapport.

d) Not accept manipulation, stand our ground without being aggressive or feeling guilty (assertive behaviour).

Examples:

A parent whose child is finding school work difficult may say: 'How come you can't even do the easy things just like the other kids?'

Husband to wife: 'We are out with people from work this evening; please try not to say anything senseless, at most just keep quiet'.

A son working with his father often hears: 'Just don't make any decisions, you always get it wrong'.

Belittling often achieves:

1) Dependency: the belittled tends to depend on others for making decisions.

The belittled often acquire:

1) Low self-esteem.
2) Fear of making mistakes and thus, need of other's approval.
3) Fear of judgement.

Parents who frequently inferiorize their children could create grounds for them to grow up feeling under-confident and indecisive.

This could be the case of 50 year old John. He claims he is unable to continue his 30-year sales activity. I am astonished. John goes on to say how his business has always been run by his father. His father has never allowed John to make decisions, always claiming him incapable of making the right ones. The father retired at eighty and moved to the coast. Now John has to call his father every time he needs to make a decision, even though he knows his father is no longer able to make them, indeed he has recently made some very poor ones. John knows what he *should* do, yet he is afraid of goofing up, he procrastinates, and when he finally makes his decision, he is unconvinced of his choice.

Often in blaming or inferiorizing we justify our behaviour saying that we do it for the other's own good. This may be so, but in any case, it is not a pleasant feeling when we are blamed or put down.

Being faced with unpredictable behaviour is another source of discomfort. This type of behaviour is not considered exactly a manipulative strategy; however it does produce an elevated sense of discomfort.

Look at the example: A father arrives home after work and begins to play with his young son. The boy soon learns, and every time his father returns, he runs towards him ready for play. The father usually picks him up and smiles. Today is different: Dad has had a bad day at work; he steams through the door and brushes past the boy.

Here we have a situation where the same behaviour is indiscriminately rewarded or punished. The boy no longer knows how to behave; does he run towards or away from his father? He learns how to observe his father's non-verbal communication, checks to see if he is happy, and only then decides whether or not to run towards him. This endless 'checking out the situation' leads to a permanent state of anxiety.

I have been invited to friends' for dinner. Before we eat,

I chat with my friend and his wife while their six year old is busy drawing. After about fifteen minutes the boy brings the drawing to his mother. She takes a look, compliments the boy and asks him to draw another before returning to the kitchen to finish preparing the meal. Sure enough, the boy brings his new drawing to mum who this time pushing him off saying 'Not now, can't you see I'm busy'. The boy returns to the living room, scrunches up the drawing into a ball and throw it at his father. The father smacks the boy and sends him to his room. From the room we hear loud noises of the boy taking it out on his toys. The father looks at me and says 'See how he gets so up-tight for nothing'

Let's look at what happened:

1) The boy shows a drawing to his mother as we are talking.
2) The mother rewards the boy and invites him to make another drawing.
3) The boy returns with a new drawing.
4) The mother, otherwise busy, sends the boy away (perceived punishment).
5) The boy has been rewarded and punished for the same behaviour.
6) He feels frustrated.
7) The boy throws the drawing at the father and is slapped,
8) The boy goes to his room and takes it out on his toys (dislocated aggressiveness).

When the same behaviour is indiscriminately rewarded and punished, we cannot know how to behave. This creates huge discomfort which could follow in either aggressive or passive behaviour.

We see how the boy has started showing dislocated aggressiveness. This is typical; the classic example is when we are picked on by our boss at work then later take it out on our spouse or children.

Social Skills

Knowing how to handle a conversation, holding eye contact while we speak, telling someone we like them, interrupting a group conversation at the right time and speaking in public are all social skills and if we have them, they make social interaction a better experience.

We issue behaviour all the time which involves:

1) The motor system. When we observe someone we can easily note the tone of voice, aggressive behaviour or self-exclusion.
2) The physiological-emotional system. In adverse situations, we activate an emotional response: increased heartbeat, sweating, stomach cramps.
3) The cognitive system. This is our 'baggage' of suppositions and beliefs.

Example: We are on our way to an important appointment for work. We can issue two types of response sequences:

Sequence I:
a) Cognitive – I think: 'I've got to look good; I need this job; I hope this guy isn't the bossy type'.
b) Emotional - We break out in a sweat even before the appointment. We feel very uncomfortable.
c) Motor - We are tongue-tied and inappropriate at the interview.

Sequence II:

a) Cognitive - I think: 'I'll present myself and hear what this guy has to say'.
b) Emotional - No physiological response.
c) Motor - We make our offer and listen to the reply. We check if the reply is what we hoped for.

Often negative expectations activate negative emotional responses to influence our performance.

Social behaviour is result of learning. This learning may be through imitation of our parents', peers or other significant adult (e.g. our school teachers). A child is shaped by the environment he lives in and the learned social behaviours will be reproduced in other social situations. The child with an aggressive father may become passive or aggressive, but rarely assertive.

We have seen how some manipulative strategies tend to inhibit those who suffer them. A child who has been systematically poor-mouthed by the father will often become passive. The child who observes his father being aggressive and gaining success or respect through this behaviour, could indeed end up behaving in the same way.

The more we are able to control our own behaviour and thus handle situations without discomfort, the better our lives become. We should be able to feel comfortable when we are:

— Alone or in company.
— Under criticism or in receiving compliments.
— Ignored or the centre of attention in group situations.
— In any social environment.
— In company with 'ordinary' or 'important' people.
— In company with passive and aggressive types.

There are many other typical situations which cause discomfort. However, the only way to get over this is to deal with it. To face up to discomfort we need to get a handle on certain behaviour types. In the next chapter we will see what skills are needed to do this. It is obvious that we all prefer avoiding prickly situations, but avoidance tactics leave you ingrained in a vicious circle which is undeniably difficult to escape.

Assertive Communication

Non-verbal communication

You know the feeling when someone never looks you in the eye. Their gaze wanders everywhere else but in your direction and you can't seem to grasp their attention. It makes you uneasy and unsure if what you are saying has actually been taken in. The skill of making eye contact is an important part of non-verbal social behaviour.

Passive types usually find it hard to maintain eye contact. The feeling of being observed can be interpreted as 'I'm being judged'. The very thought creates discomfort and to lessen it, non-verbal interaction (eye contact) is withdrawn.

Others avoid prolonged eye contact as they fear being 'invasive'. Eye contact is usually used twice as much in listening than speaking.

People who are able to maintain good eye contact appear as being open, confident and self- assured. Eye contact can convey 'I like you' to someone we find attractive. We really don't need words to show our interest in someone.

Eye contact is one important aspect of interpersonal communication. Other non-verbal behaviours are listed below:

— Facial expression.
— Gesticulation.
— Body posture/stance.
— Management of inter-personal space.
— Voice tone and volume.
— Physical contact.
— In sync/on the same wavelength.

Facial expression

Our expressions give some fairly precise information about what we are thinking; it is one way of manifesting emotion. Good actors do just that. Think of actor Jim Carey and how cleverly he used facial mimicry to communicate feelings and emotions in the roles he played.

People with lesser social skills actually show less expression. Passive or aggressive individuals often have a motionless air about them. Verbal behaviour should correspond to corresponding facial mimicry.

A while ago I was training one of my clients how to give compliments. He reckoned he had never done so with his wife. At his return shortly after, he reported that his instructions hadn't worked. On asking for elucidation he explained how he had tried to tell his wife he really liked her in a new dress, and she had replied: 'Oh really? How can I take you seriously with that expression on your face? You'd be better off keeping quiet'. Obviously, his facial expression and the compliment were not aligned.

Our expression highlights and accentuates our thoughts, feelings and sensations. Often highly self-controlled people tend to a deadpan expression in their inability to communicate feelings. This can result in awkwardness, trust is lost and therefore, the quality of rapport.

Having good social skills mean we are able to discern subtle emotional states from facial expression. Assertive types can learn how to observe and decode the emotions behind the expression. Aggressive types, in their disregard for others, and passive types in their awkwardness during social exchange, avoid observation altogether.

Gesticulation

By gesticulation we mean movement of hands or other parts of the body.

When we speak we use our hands to emphasize or make clear what we are describing. Our hand gestures can serve two purposes:

1) Description: Gestures provide information on action, shape or size.
1) Emphasis: To accentuate and highlight parts of dialogue.

In very tense circumstances, gesticulation is no longer functional to communication. In uncomfortable situations we might wring our hands or fiddle with a pen, a ring etc. It is usually indication of significant social anxiety.

Head movement is also relevant in communication. We can encourage, approve, acquiesce or indicate exactly the contrary.

Body Posture

When we are feeling comfortable in social situations our physical bodies relax; we sit back lopsidedly; our hands, neck and face are stress-free. On the contrary, a rigid, symmetrical posture indicates body tension.

We can also manifest superior or inferior behaviours with body posture.

Let's see a classic example of superiority. We are in the office; the boss calls an employee to his desk and even before conversation begins, we see how the top man leans back, chin raised, fixed gaze and not even a shadow of a smile. These are behavioural non-verbal manipulative strategies aimed at creating awkwardness and a claim to 'right of position'.

Management of inter-personal space

For sure you have experienced the feeling of someone taking over and at you. As you strike up conversation, the person moves towards you; you start backing off and they undauntedly creep closer. You are uncomfortable; you end up back against the wall. You likely are talking to an Arab or an aggressive. In a western culture, for conversation purposes the best distance between you and the other is around one metre; we get closer only if we need to share something confidential. In other cultures such as in Arab countries, the distance is much less. Passive types tend to keep further away while aggressive types tend to get closer.

Voice tone and volume

We communicate our mood and emotions or stress parts of speech using tone and volume. Aggressive people raise the volume or adopt a severe tone if criticizing. Anxiousness will cause rapid speech, while passive types will keep their tone low, often inadequate for the subject matter, but however expressing their mood.

Physical contact

Physical contact usually aims to establish a feeling of intimacy and solidarity. With a friend, a hand shake, a hug or linking arms, will go to easing conversation, providing the person we are talking to is not suffering social anxiety, in which case it could create discomfort.

Some types of physical contact are not functional to better communication; most people do not enjoy having their tie adjusted or having the stray hair brushed off their jacket while conversing.

Synchronization

You will recognise the interrupter; he's the one that butts in every time you speak. Or you might remember a time in company when you could never find the right moment to say your bit. These are examples of bad timing. For communication to continue it is necessary to synchronize the verbal component between two or more individuals. Timing is coordinated by non-verbal signals which indicate when we must end our speech allow space for the next speaker.

To have good communication we must be careful of the feedback. Passive types will often find it challenging to enter into the conversation. Aggressive types won't leave space for others to speak. Key to good communication is to observe facial expression to recognize if we are being understood or if what we are saying maintains interest. Constant attention of feedback in this way allows us to modify accordingly the form or content of or words.

How non-verbal communication works

Some social psychologists have found that in communicating attitudes of superiority, hostility or friendship, the result of non-verbal communication is about four times more than the result you get through verbal behaviour. So the main function of non-verbal behaviour is to express mood and emotions related to social interaction. Obviously, in communication and for good interaction non-verbal behaviour must be congruent with verbal behaviour. A person can declare his friendship and yet on meeting, show no form of non-verbal pleasure; no smiling, avoidance of physical contact. This is incongruent.

In communicating, our appearance may play an important role alongside non-verbal behaviour; our clothing, hairstyle, the way we walk, move, or sit and so on. People with good non-verbal skills are better at discerning retroactive information for use in the interpersonal situation. There are two main skills involved in gathering non-verbal information:

1) Decoding intention, emotions, mood and interpersonal approach.
2) Understanding the social status and role of the other.

New encounters always bring some degree of trepidation. Feeding our apprehension is usually fear of judgement or fretfulness in our attempts to make a good impression. So how do we lessen this feeling of awkwardness without resorting to avoidance tactics? The following steps should help:

1) Learn to distinguish behaviour styles. Start from a situation that is not too emotionally engaging (otherwise it will be impossible). Observe the non-verbal behaviour of the people around you. Recognize if they are aggressive, passive or assertive. Identify their style of interaction and observe how they look at others, their facial expressions, and so on. Identify their role and social status. Television can be helpful; watch a talk show, here it's easy to identify the social behaviour we preferably *do not* want to copy.

2) Identify those areas of non-verbal behaviour where you might be lacking and start self-training. If eye contact is your issue, practice holding eye contact initially with people you are comfortable with. Try it out later on with someone who puts you a tad out of your comfort zone, for example an aggressive type. It will be difficult at first, but the more you practice the easier it gets, it is important to do it gradually, moving on only when you are in full control of each step.

In training there should be a constant interaction between discriminatory learning and increase of skills. You can also practice in front of a mirror or better still, film yourself; imagine that you are going to practice, let's say, standoffishness: film yourself, then check back to see if you are really communicating this attitude.

A representative, a client of mine, had huge issues with the arrogant types he frequently did business with. He felt sorely inadequate, so much so he could rarely express himself. He learned to distinguish their non-verbal behaviour then modelled the same on himself. I caught up with him a few weeks later and he reported: 'I went to visit one of those guys who used to make me feel really uncomfortable; right on cue from behind the desk he starts the full non-verbal ritual. This time, chuckling to myself, I recognized the whole scenario, just as I had practiced; him leaning back on the chair, half-closed eyes; chin up and in a toneless voice 'What are you offering this time?'

Once we start recognizing these sequences of behaviour, we are well on the way to reducing our feelings of discomfort.

Verbal communication

Having good social skills implies having assertive-type verbal communication. Remember that assertive people do not show aggressive behaviour, nor do they suffer others. The assertive type, together with suitable non-verbal communication skills in various situations is also able to:

1) Openly express an opinion.
2) Take and make compliments.
3) Make or refuse requests.
4) Manage manipulative criticism without discomfort or feeling guilty.
5) Be a good, attentive listener.
7) Accept other people's point of view.

These skills can be acquired through precise interactive verbal behaviours. The main techniques that are traditionally part of assertive verbal behaviour are:

1) Assertive conversation techniques.
2) Positive expression.
3) Making or refusing requests.
4) Stuck record technique.
5) Fogging.
6) Negative assertion.
7) Negative enquiry.

Assertive communication techniques

Take a look at the conversation between two friends:

— 'So you went to the seaside again on holiday this year?'
— 'Yes, just like last year.'
— 'Did you do much sailing?'
— 'Yes.'

As we can see, the answers give very little information and it's not easy to handle a conversation of this type. Often conversations start with this type of 'closed question', leaving space only for 'yes' or 'no' answers. Also the question: 'So you went to the seaside again on holiday this year?' The answer can only be 'yes' or 'no'.

Insisting along these lines greatly restricts conversation ultimately drawing it to a close. These types of questions may be good for starters, but after they must be followed by 'open questions'. Open questions start with 'Why...' How..? 'What..?'

Obviously questions alone cannot establish conversation; it would be like an interview!

A further skill is being able to give or receive 'free information'; the information not requested in the question. Assertive people recognize immediately from simple clues what is important or interesting to them and pay immediate attention. Attention that can also be expressed non-verbally by looking at the interlocutor in the face and nodding in agreement.

People with poor social skills have difficulty in grasping the free information. Passive people rarely give free information, believing that what they say is of no interest. In any case, even when we recognize the free information but do not want to start a discussion about that particular subject, we let it drop.

Other than giving free information, we can also communicate our lifestyle, way of thinking; we can talk about ourselves and our lives. This ability is called 'Self-opening'. We just have to be careful that this does not become just a bragging monologue, which is not assertive behaviour!

Let's take another look at the previous dialogue:

— 'So you went on holiday to the seaside again this year?' (Closed question).
— 'Yes, and I did loads of sailing' (Free information).
— 'Was the wind favourable?' (Closed question, it links to the previous free information).
— 'Well one day it was force 9, like, really wild! I was so scared; but, you know, once I got used to it, it was a real adrenalin charge. (Self-opening).
— 'Yeah, I know what you mean, I remember times when I've felt that electrifying mix of fear and excitement' (Free information and self-opening).

In this dialogue, the two friends use both free information and self-opening thus neatly communicating through verbal synchronization.

Positive expression

Openly expressing congeniality or complementing someone you are attracted to, are examples of positive expressions we often fail to convey. In such people it may cause discomfort to receive compliments. However, possessing this skill is likely to improve social contact and to create gratifying interaction.

A good manager will highlight the positive aspects of collaborators, in doing so it creates a less frustrating and more gratifying environment, thus increasing productivity. Aggressive managers tend to be more critical, using negative expressions in the hope of increasing productivity. Sadly, this type of interaction creates frustration which becomes a vicious circle: colleagues feel frustrated, they work less, produce less and are criticized more.

Making or refusing requests

Non-assertive types avoid making demands for fear of encountering refusal or the belief that it is not 'polite' to disturb others. Some are not able to accept rejection. Often there is the mistaken opinion that others have to figure out for themselves what you need. This behaviour emerges mainly in intimate relationships; between parents and children or couples.

Making requests serves to strengthen solidarity; it allows us to communicate our desires or needs.

Knowing how to refuse is actually like a mirror image of

making requests, because by refusing we declare the extent to which we are available. Making and refusing requests gives clear information about how we are.

Stuck record technique

A friend asks a favour and we refuse. The friend induces guilt with phrases like: 'I didn't expect *you* to refuse...' In these cases a simple refusal is not sufficient. Here you need the stuck record technique: Calmly repeat your point of view using the same words for every manipulative strategy that is offered and do not get further involved.

In these situations it is vital not to justify your refusal. The stuck record technique is, in this situation, a procedure that protects us from manipulation. It is also important to remember our goal so as not to be dragged into 'irrelevant logic' of others. Using the stuck record will help keep focused on the goal.

This works brilliantly when you want to get rid of the pushy salesperson. Just gently reiterate: 'No thank you, I'm not interested'. It is a useful and simple technique, I started using it after buying a significant amount of soap, deodorant and cigarette lighters that I regularly did not use or need. The same technique can be used in different contexts, for example, when asserting our rights. If we bought a faulty device and it is our right to have it replaced. The seller may try to pull a sharp one; all we have to do is calmly insist.

Fogging

This skill allows us to accept criticism by admitting and accepting that there may be some truth behind it. If our critic is generally an aggressive type, contradiction will only foment their aggressiveness, leading to futile perpetuation of the discussion. In these cases good lines are: 'Probably you are right' or 'I see what you mean.' Paraphrasing can also be useful, it allows for the criticized to play for time and reduce the discomfort, meanwhile, the one is dispensing criticism feels understood. We see the following dialogue:

— 'How come you are never there when I need you?' (Manipulative criticism).
— 'You say that when you need me I'm never around, right?' (Paraphrase, acceptance of other with no justification).

Once our critic has 'calmed down', you can start a dialogue which aims to understand what they expect from us and make clear what we are able to give them.

Negative assertion

With negative assertion we mean the statement with which we admit our mistake, declaring total agreement with our critic. Aggressive people tend not to recognize their mistakes and do not apologize. Assertive behaviour is to acknowledge a mistake and apologize, for example:

— 'You were rather sharp with John yesterday, weren't you?'
— 'You're right, I see that now, I'll call and apologize' (Negative assertion).

Often critics will give only generalized information which prevents understanding of what went wrong and subsequently how to find improvement or a remedy. Negative inquiry calls for a more precise and detailed criticism. If the criticism is manipulative, negative enquiry puts an end to manipulation, bringing the other to turn criticism into a constructive dialogue. The following example is between a manager and his new secretary:

MANAGER: This letter is rubbish! (Manipulative criticism).

SECRETARY: Can you please show me where it is wrong? (Negative enquiry).

MANAGER: Do I really have to tell you such trivialities? (Manipulative criticism).

SECRETARY: Can you please show me where I went wrong? (Negative enquiry and stuck record).

MANAGER: (Pointing to where in the letter) Here, this part (Constructive criticism).

SECRETARY: Is there anything else that is not clear? (Negative enquiry).

MANAGER: No, the rest is fine.

In normal conversation many techniques are used together.

Handling Criticism

How do we behave when criticized? Does it depend on what the criticism is? We have seen two type of criticism: constructive and manipulative.

Constructive criticism contains useful information, helping dialogue and exchange of opinion.

Manipulative criticism contains general assertions on our behaviour or performance. It is unproductive as it does not contain any useful information to correct our errors. They may make us feel guilty or inferior (see 'Manipulative strategies').

Passive types who put up with manipulative criticism will tend to silence or justify their behaviour. In this way criticism will persist. If the same criticism is directed to an aggressive type they will probably counter-attack, creating conflict. It will become a totally barren exchange leading to resentment and rivalry.

So if our criticism is constructive, how will our passive and aggressive types react?

Let's imagine a friend with an issue to solve. We might try to help with some advice of the 'Why don't you try to ...?" kind. Our friend may reply: 'I know what to do; I don't need your help' (Aggressive behaviour). Or perhaps he won't reply at all, nor ask for further explanation; we realize he is uncomfortable receiving help, perhaps feeling judged or criticised (Passive behaviour). Either way, we stop giving information. The dialogue cannot continue if we are confronted or if we feel the other is ill at ease. See how non-assertive types do not discern between constructive or manipulative criticism:

Criticism	Behaviour	Reply	Communication
M			
A	PASSIVE	Escape	Continuous
N			
I			
P			
U	AGGRESSIVE	Attack	Continuous
L			
A			
T			
I	ASSERTIVE	Discerns defensive verbal skills	Cancelled
V			
E			

Criticism	Behaviour	Reply	Communication
C			
O	PASSIVE	Escape	Cancelled
N			
S			
T			
R	AGGRESSIVE	Attack	Cancelled
U			
C			
T			
I	ASSERTIVE	Discerns solicited verbal skills	Continuous
V			
E			

We can see how assertive individuals discern the type of criticism used. So if you encounter manipulative criticism, use defensive techniques such as fogging, paraphrase or negative assertion. Doing so will cancel the unwanted behaviour. Subsequently clear information is required (Negative enquiry), thus turning into constructive criticism. Constructive criticism is always accepted, indeed, it will also require further input (Negative enquiry).

Here's a dialogue between two friends at work:

— 'You realize you can't be trusted, don't you?' (Manipulative criticism).
— 'You say I'm not trustworthy (Paraphrase). So what is it about my behaviour that isn't trusting? (Negative enquiry)'.
— 'You're always overdue for deadlines.'
— 'That is true; I'm never on time (Negative assertion). If there is anything else I do that bothers you, please feel free to tell me (Negative enquiry), better to get things straight right away'.
— 'No, just your timeliness.'
— 'Thank you for telling me, it will help. In the future, you could help me by reminding me a couple of days before the deadline.'
— 'I'll do that for sure.'

Let's take a closer look at the skills required for good assertive social behaviour under criticism:

1) Distinguish type of criticism (constructive or manipulative).
2) Use verbal skills to block manipulation.
3) Avoid justification or excuse, recognize when at fault.

4) Accept other points of view.
5) Solicit eventual criticism encouraging use of straightforward language.

It is indeed an arduous task to completely rebuild a model of a person with good assertive skills. It means successfully mastering verbal and nonverbal behaviour, being non-judgmental, accepting other points of view, managing criticism and so forth. We have studied the assertive type in their observable behaviour. And it doesn't end here, so the next question is: How to they manage negative emotional responses and how do they think?

When a friend is successful, and we are not, resentment can set in creating frustration when things don't quite go as we expected. Some of our thinking can trigger negative emotional responses and affect our behaviour. Rationally we can say: 'I must try to be assertive (with person), not aggressive.' But if, before meeting *that* person, we feel a grudge, it is very unlikely we are going to be assertive. We can control our verbal behaviour, but probably not the non-verbal part. It is unlikely we will present looking cool, with a 'willing to talk' attitude. A hint of aggressiveness and our presumed self-control will vanish.

So does an assertive type never get the grump? With practice it becomes increasingly difficult to get angry. In any case, if we believe we need to state a point, we can do it without blaming or putting down, but simply by stating what's going on, without experiencing anger or resentment. In the following chapters we will look at typical thought patterns which aim to make us feel miserable, and we will see how to overcome those obstacles and start feeling good. The goal to feel good is not easy to achieve. It's easier to feel bad.

Expectations

Creating expectations

We start a new job; meet someone new, it's normal to have expectations. Faced with any new event we can act in two ways:

1) Create massive expectations.
2) Create minimal expectations.

In the first case we assume we are able to control all events and imagine everything will go as we presume. When despite our efforts that does not happen, it brings a sense of frustration that can manifest as aggressive behaviour especially if we attribute our failure to others. In the second case, we believe we can never control events and therefore it is useless bothering. In this case we think: 'Whatever I do, even if it's okay, it's not up to me, so why even try?' This thinking leads to passivity, we are 'on hold', and dependent on others. This state of helplessness will eventually lead to depression.

When a job or relationship is consolidated in time, we hope it will remain so. We are used to giving the same sequence of responses in a given situation, if the situation changes we do not have the means or knowledge to respond appropriately, we feel uncomfortable, wanting the situation to return as it was previously. When this does not happen we become aggressive, or we get depressed. We'll see some cases where false expectations can create a state of deep distress.

Expectations in relationships

Claudia is forty, married for fifteen years and has a thirteen year old daughter. She works with her husband Kevin, who works in the company Claudia owns. Their relationship is not going well, Kevin has a twenty-five year old lover, and he's at home only at meal times. Claudia cannot come to terms with her husband's transformation. She declares: 'It's true I have always made the decisions at home and work which was always fine for Kevin. He never said it wasn't alright. Of course I get aggressive with him!'

Claudia approaches this issue by behind a guilt-inducing silence in the hope of ending the relationship.

I ask what her marriage was like before Kevin had a lover. She replied: 'We never really communicated, after years of marriage I'd got used to it. We ate in silence then watched TV. We've never had any tender moments, a hug or a kiss'.

Claudia had never expected her husband's new behaviour. Although their relationship wasn't very satisfactory, she had grown used to it. Her world has gone horribly pear-shaped; she is depressed, takes tranquillizers, has a poor appetite and sleeps badly. This makes her even more aggressive; she can't compete with her husband. So everybody is unhappy, Claudia certainly is the worse off; her husband has more space outside of the marriage scenario. We can see that Claudia's strategies have not worked. It is absolutely necessary that *WE DO NOT EXPECT OTHERS TO BEHAVE THE WAY WE WANT.* So many of us try to change their partner and put all our efforts in trying to do so. At first we are passive, trying our utmost to satisfy our partner in the hope that they will do the same. When this does not give results, we get exasperated. As a result we either become extremely passive or slip into aggressiveness. Our thoughts and behaviour, being always focused on the other, shroud insight on our behaviour. It is crucial to shift our attention inwards, towards ourselves. We are the ones who are suffering. Our aim is to reach a state of wellbeing. Understandably, we don't want to be unhappy, but it is absurd to believe we can be happy in the never-ending vice of trying to modify someone else's behaviour (because impossible) so *OTHER PEOPLE ARE NOT TO MODIFY.* Once we can accept this affirmation, everything anyone else does is acceptable. We must put ourselves first. Selfish you say? Is trying to bend others to our will for self-gratification not selfish?

Claudia commits two cognitive errors which are based on the following suppositions: my husband has to change and my behaviour is right. So let's see what she could do better. First and foremost, she must avoid being aggressive towards her husband - her husband must find his wife's company more gratifying than his lover's. Let's presume that Claudia has changed and she's now kind and attentive to her husband.

You probably think it is nigh on impossible to be nice to someone who has committed adultery. For sure, when you are with your transgressor, your first response is emotional. We are nervous, angry and tongue tied and it is exactly here that we return to our old behaviour, in this case, aggressiveness. When we decide to change we meet immediate difficulty. We try to accommodate our partner, we are kind and keep our attacks at bay, but we are looking for a rapid change in our partner, and if nothing happens we think: 'I'm making a big effort to change, but he's doing nothing and I'm taking all the responsibility, which can't be right'.

At this point, perhaps, just stop for a moment and ask yourself if you really want to recover the relationship, are you prepared to take on all the responsibility, at such a high price, and expect nothing in return? True, it's not easy to think this way, is it?

If we decide we want to recover the relationship, we must expect to pay the price and realize that there may be no gain. I remember one of my clients affirmed: 'I'm going to do everything I can to recover my relationship, If I don't at least I can say I did all I could'.

If, on the other hand, we decide to leave, will we be able to survive on our own?

For some of us life is better in an unhappy relationship rather than being alone. Claudia spends many totally ungratifying evenings with her husband. There is no rapport, verbal or physical. However, she believes it is better with him than being alone. It 'costs' her less. So what has Claudia gained from her aggressiveness? A brief victory; this is only my guess, as I have no further information about their relationship. Her husband has returned after breaking off with the lover.

Either way, we should remember that *WE MUST NOT BE DE-SPONDENT*. Nonetheless, be careful of this affirmation. The worst scenario would be to launch ourselves into another relationship. This is what happened to my friend Josh. He ended his marriage a while ago, after eight years' together. A decidedly 'lively' marriage, with frequent bouts of aggressiveness, during which time, the couple managed to destroy several plates (usually about four or five at a time). An 'Impossible marriage' he declared. I don't know his wife's opinion. Once separated, Josh went through many challenging moments. After years of living in company he suffered from loneliness, returning to an empty house, watching TV in the company of a glass of whisky. It may seem strange to think he felt so miserable on his own, after years of unhappiness in the company of his wife.

Unable to bear the solitude, he thinks he needs some company. He starts dating, and after about a month after his separation, he tells me he has found the 'right' person. He moves in with his date and so begins a new relationship. Josh has embarked on a new relationship to escape the misery of being alone; so far so good. There is only one important detail: Josh is incapable of making a choice.

His anxiety forced him to start a new relationship. It would have been better if he had found a way to be on his own without the distress, so that he wouldn't have rushed into a decision. Josh expects this new liaison to go well and that his friend shares his way of thinking. For some months it does, it is a peaceful co-existence. But the lady-friend starts asserting herself, she needs independence. Josh is not expecting this; to him a relationship is 'total'. Josh returns to the same behaviour that created the contrasts he had with his wife; he becomes aggressive. They break up after four months and the story is repeated. He is miserable on his own so he finds another date. We can clearly see Josh's cognitive error when he claims: 'I am happy only if I am in a totally dependent relationship'. To obtain such engrossment he tends to placate his partners, so really his involvement is only his alone.

There is a common denominator in Claudia and Josh's behaviour. They both start from their operating level rather than from the other persons'. If a friend is able to give ten we should not expect one hundred. If we are convinced we give more and we consider one hundred our level of performance, you should not expect an equal performance. There is often a belief that we give more than we take.

Still on the theme of false expectations, we are often convinced that our partners should always behave like we do, even under different circumstances. A client of mine stated: 'When I am alone with my husband, he is often silent and withdrawn. If I ask him what's up his reply is 'Nothing' and returns to his silence. When friends come round he is totally different, he is cheerful, and talkative, even with the really boring ones. It is like my husband is two different people. With me he is introverted and uncommunicative; with friends he is always cheerful. Why doesn't he treat me like he does with our friends?'

For sure it is not pleasing to see your partner behave so ambiguously. It is disorienting to witness such a rapid personality change. So what can we do? Firstly we must be careful around telling ourselves that you want it to be different, this gets you into the 'I want them to change' trap. We forget that others are not to be changed. Remember it is we who are hurting inside.

Instead of focussing attention on the partner, take a look at our own behaviour. We will realize that we too change behaviour in different situation. The environment plays an important role. With a partner we suffer, we become aggressive towards each other. It takes just a tiny change in the environment and our behaviour modifies. It is true that some of us are more apparent, and thus behaviour modification is more noticeable. But remember that *EVERYONE IS UNDER ENVIRONMENTAL PRESSURE.* My client had no particular difficulty in accepting this statement, after observing her own behaviour in various social situations, she realized that her husband was not being 'ambiguous' for the sole purpose of creating difficulty between the two of them. She learned to accept.

Obviously, you can accept behaviour which has a lower price to pay. In any case, whinging about it is useless. What really matters are the procedures. Also, in couple situations, postponing decisions is useless; all it does is make us feel worse. I remember, uncomfortably, a client of mine way back in the sixties. She had been an elementary school teacher for thirty years, a gentlewoman, and truly kind. She married thirty five years ago, but had wanted to end the marriage after only a few months. The husband was an introvert, paying her little or no attention. Sometimes he shook her up. But she was expecting her first child. She hoped that with the new-born her husband would change. But this did not happen. Even the advent of the second child did not change her husband. Now, sixty years old, she takes stock of her life. She says: 'I understand, now, that I've thrown my life away, I'm tied to a man with whom I have nothing in common.'

Creating false expectations

The fear of losing someone often make us behave so as to please the other. We tell them what they want to hear. This would be absolutely fine as long as creating false expectations does not work against us. Sometimes, if we think that a person is important for our well-being we place ourselves below them. We depend, therefore, on this person. Continuing the relationship, we feel oppressed: the relationship becomes, for us, an adversity. You start blaming your partner for your own state of discomfort. You *must* change the way you think. We have to accept the following statement: IT IS OUR OWN

FAULT IF WE ARE UNHAPPY. It's hard to accept, isn't it? This type of statement is positive as it pushes us to look at our own faults, not those of others. If we continually seek to identify their negative aspects we suffer because we can, in fact, do nothing to change them. This is the case of fifty year old Frank, separated for a year with two sons of twenty and eighteen, both living with his wife. He has always been a womanizer and has always been unfaithful. He does not feel remotely guilty about his behaviour. His one blunder, however, is that he does not provide his partners with the truth. Still he likes having romantic relationships. He has a girlfriend and once again he has created false expectations, telling her that any worthwhile relationship is monogamous. Everything has been going well in these few months; they are always together, spending many a pleasant weekend. But 'saturation' is lurking for Frank; he begins to feel closed in. He has elaborated some feeble excuses for when he hitches up with some new lady-friend. He tells me: 'The situation is worse than when I was married, I feel I'm being controlled, I just don't understand women, they are all the same, after a while they all get possessive. Frank has made a few mistakes.

The first is a faulty self-assessment: he believes he is monogamous when he isn't.

The second is his creating expectations with his partner that he cannot keep.

This is not assertive behaviour, it is passive-aggressive. He is passive when he gives misguiding information to his partner, so as not to lose her, and aggressive, because he blames the partner for his discomfort.

Now let's see an assertive behaviour:

Frank should have said to his prospective partner something like: 'I really like you, but I don't want to get tied,

I need you to know that I have other relations'. Frank immediately objects to this: 'If I say that they'll run away, no one can accept that kind of claim'. This is probably true; but for sure if our communication is clear we avoid creating the frustration that otherwise, false expectations lead to. And when our partner feels frustrated we too feel bad. It may happen that despite having given correct information, both partners create false expectations. If the partner does not accept our point of view, then it becomes the other's problem. A friend tells me she'd been dating someone she really likes for about two weeks. She'd told him that she also liked to hang out with other guys. Two or three days passed and her date had called, nice as ever, to organize the weekend. He'd asked where she'd been the night before. She'd replied that the deal was not to ask questions; and then said it was his right to ask, but it was his problem to handle the answer. He had insisted, so she told him she'd slept with another guy. His reaction was immediate and aggressive. She then told him 'I'm sorry you feel bad, my telling the truth is now a problem for you'.

You might think that a bit of deviousness is required now and again. In any case the rule is: *DON'T ASK QUESTIONS IF YOU CAN'T HANDLE THE ANSWERS.*

Often, when asking questions we create expectations. We may choose to accept or refuse the answers we get. But what use is there in not accepting the answers? Take a look at the following:

1-a) Question...?
The answer is what we expect.
We accept it.
We are fine.

1-b) Question…?
The answer is what we expect.
We don't accept it. We think: 'He only said that to keep me happy, it's not what he really thinks' (cognitive error: our interpretation?).
We feel awkward.
We ask more questions, but cannot accept any answer and continue in our discomfort.

2-a) Question…?
The answer is not what we expect.
We accept it.
We are fine.

2-b) Question…?
The answer is not what we expect.
We don't accept it and think: 'That's a strange (wrong) way of thinking!' (Cognitive error: 'Mine is the only right way to think'). We feel awkward.
We ask more questions. We want to find some sort of common ground.
We cannot agree to everything. We are dissatisfied.
We feel discomfort.

Observe dialogue that followed a call between my client and her friend:

HER: 'I'm sorry you were upset about what I said I had done the other evening, but I don't like making up excuses'.
HIM: 'I can't understand how it is you say you like being with me, and then you go and sleep with another guy. Of course I'm upset, you are confusing'.

HER: 'I do like being with you, you are a really nice guy.'

The friend had deduced from her line 'I like hanging out with you' that she meant him and *only* him. However this is his version of reality and we can see how it is causing him problems. She reiterates that she like being with him, she did not say he is the only one she like hanging out with. In this case it is difficult to reach some sort of agreement. They see things very differently. In similar cases, if this point of view accepted, it is probably due to fear of losing the relationship.

Friendship

All the statements we have used so far to describe couples in various situations can also be applied to describe friendships. We see how in the same way the fear of losing a friend leads us to create false expectations.

Let's go back to Claudia. She tells me: 'I've lost all of my friends, I've been let down so many times, only recently I've ended a friendship because I realized my friend only called me if she needed something. That's not what friends are for'. Yet when asked, she insisted that she got on well with her friend who is a happy-go-lucky type.

In the same way as in her relationship, Claudia had not considered her friends' operating level. The friend is positive, cheerful, outgoing and great in company. For Claudia the negative aspect is that she rarely calls and if she does, it is only to ask for favours. Remember that we can only take what the other is able to give. Claudia is happy to see her friend, yet she has closed the friendship because the friend does not behave as she believes friends should, or rather in a way that Claudia has framed the meaning of friendship. One of Claudia's errors is her inability to manage her friend's requests; she never refuses the friend's call to ask for something, even at a high price. Obviously, it is inconvenient to do something we don't want to. We thus are irritated by whoever it is asking us costly favours. This is *our* problem. We assume: 'You can't turn a friend down', should be modified to '*OTHERS HAVE A RIGHT TO ASK, AND IT IS OUR EQUAL RIGHT TO REFUSE*'. If we cannot to do this we expect others never to refuse and when this doesn't happen, the friendship will end. Often we distinguish the 'true' friends as those you can always count on.

Let's see where the cognitive error lies. We tend to expect an immediate positive response from our 'true friends'. The reasoning is 'all or nothing'. This behaviour actually characterizes adolescence, the age of great affections and great disappointments.

When disappointment is constant, as in Claudia's case, we become adverse to the friendship. Our expectations have been shattered time and time again. This sparks off the 'undue generalization' mechanism, phrases like: 'Obviously they are not real friends and sooner or later they let you down', roll off our tongues. The generalizations Frank made were of the type: 'Women are all the same, they set you up, and then they get possessive'. These types of thought processes irremediably lead to isolation. Not that isolation is necessarily negative, however if we don't like being in solitude, we need to find a remedy, therefore we must ask ourselves 'Where did I go wrong? Obviously if we withdraw from society for long periods of time we lose the habit of communicating with others.

One of my clients, Luciano, did just that. He is twenty-five and works as a teller in the bank. His daily routine is always the same. Eight hours work then he barricades himself in his room to play music. He has no friends, male or female, nor has he established any kind of relationship with his work colleagues. If his job and his music were sufficient he'd be fine. He tells me: 'I want a girlfriend and I'd like some friends too. I haven't got any right now because I find their conversation is really boring and women's conversation so banal.' Luciano probably strikes you for his elevated self- esteem. He actually tells me that he is waiting for the 'right' girl and the 'right' friends to miraculously appear. The fact is he is totally lacking in social skills. He is unable to initiate conversation, answers only if questioned and, if someone of the female sex approaches, he gets so anxious he can barely speak. In this case, rather than cognitive error, Luciano's is a total lack of skills. There is also a sort of cognitive avoidance in his consideration of others as uninteresting. Whichever way we look at it, simply modifying this assumption will not be sufficient for him to be able to acquire the skills he lacks.

Self-assessment and creating false expectations

I'm gorgeous...I'm rich...I'm intelligent. Where does this super-assessment take us? It takes us to believing that we deserve everything.

A forty-five year old lady, widow of ten years, tells me that she can't find a partner. She explains that it is essential to have a 'serious' relationship. She talks about her marriage: 'My husband was a good man (often when they start like this it is because they can't find any really positive aspects) and I think he really cared for me. But I must admit we were two very different people. My parents had warned me that our differences would have created problems, and indeed they did. Although he wasn't a businessman, he started a business that almost totally collapsed. We avoided the worst thanks to my family stepping in economically. I couldn't rely on him at all.

Now let's see how the lady sees herself. She knows she is an attractive woman from a rich family. She also considers herself thoughtful, intelligent and arty. Her husband was not able to meet her expectations, which have not diminished with the passing years.

When she meets someone new, she observes them closely. She is ready to gather every negative aspect that, as always, with a little 'good will' you can always find in someone. The lady explains that her reasoning is based on the 'All or Nothing' principle.

Let's see where this way of thinking gets us. The lady has a high self-opinion, and starting from this as gauge, seeks an adequate partner. When she thinks she has found the right man, and he is always her age, intelligent, rich and good looking, it turns out that the gentleman in question does not pay her the slightest bit of attention. 'I don't understand' - said the lady - 'When a man reaches his fifties, instead their looking at women her own age, they start ogling women twenty years younger, even if the young things have very little to give. It is so true that older men lose their dignity. It's not right flirting with younger women'. Often an erroneous self-assessment creates expectations. The sense is this: If I'm worth 100, I expect a partner who is worth 100. That's what my client meant by 'everything.' Since she doesn't get the 'everything' she switches to 'nothing.' Of course there is no problem if we are happy with 'nothing'. However, having nothing in this case seems to be equally unacceptable. My question is how come we don't lower our 'requirements' or make a compromise since we can't have what we want?

There are two cognitive errors:

1) Too much attention to the 'other' as they are presumed to be the ones at fault. Consider: 'It is so true that older men lose their dignity'. Therefore, no modification in the self-assessment.
2) Living in the wait of the 'right' partner.

Expectations in daily life

At the traffic light

We are in the car, waiting at the red light. We are in a hurry. It seems that it takes forever to turn green. We are getting irritated. The more we tense up the faster our heart rate. The light turns green, a moment of relax, only to repeat exactly the same at the next light. If we can see the next one in the distance and it is green, we hope that it doesn't turn red, and so we start getting anxious again. If we see it is red we get even more irritated, because we are in a hurry. Now the traffic light has become our undaunted enemy.

So once again we leave home, this time we are not in a hurry. However, the first red light we spot triggers the conditioned response: traffic light = tension. We have just ruined what could have been an easy day. Like interpersonal relationships we believe the traffic light should also work according to our wishes, it should *always* be green. We need to learn how to give suitable responses to the tension that we are creating. These moments of 'pause' at the traffic lights need to be moments of relaxation. As soon as we realize that we are tensing up at the sight of a red light, I suggest you try this:

1) Squeeze the steering wheel; squeeze hard for around three seconds.
2) Breath in through your nose as you squeeze and breath out from your mouth as you relax your grip.

Your shoulders and arms should rapidly relax. Thus the red light signal becomes anchored to relaxation. Apply this regularly and you will break the vicious circle traffic light = tension, turning into a new trigger of traffic light = relaxation'. For sure at the beginning it will be hard to control our negative thoughts such as: 'I'll be late!' Why does it take so long to turn green?' 'Why doesn't the guy in front get a move on?' Remember they are only negative (and useless) thoughts which do not provide solutions, they only serve to increase our discomfort (and increase adrenalin and noradrenalin release, promoting stress).

You could try to change the negative thoughts into positive ones, such as: 'Calm down! I must keep my cool!' That is fine, but anyway the best way forward is to relax. Only once we are able to relax, you can use reassuring phrases such as: 'I do not need to get agitated.' The use of these phrases, unrelated to the relaxation, increases our tension. How many times we have we heard ouselves say 'calm down' only to result in our feeling more tense. You cannot 'just calm down' unless you know the steps required to release the tension.

The train delay

When the train is delayed or, worse still, there is a sudden strike, we get anxious. We issue behaviour similar to the traffic light scenario. But let's say in this case the emotional responses are more intense. At the traffic lights we are driving and we are not as totally passive as we are when waiting for a train. Our discomfort increases as the delay is prolonged. We try to communicate our discontent to another traveller. We seek their understanding and solidarity, helping to temporarily reduce our discomfort, which then exacerbates on hearing the announcement of a further delay. Our cognitive processes are very stimulated.

All our thoughts tend towards aggressive. As we have seen, the result of our aggressiveness is to feel discomfort. It is improbable that in these situations you can keep cool by telling yourself: 'Seeing as I can't do anything about it, it's pointless me getting upset'. In this example you can see how external events affect our behaviour. We are comfortable until they announce the train delay. Then, within seconds, we become tense and irascible. Our difficulty is to control the emotional response. Keeping cool, calm and collected in a challenging situation is what desire. On the contrary, there is nothing intentional about getting tetchy. So, if the train is late, let's try for once to say: 'Keep calm, keep cool'. If we can keep control, even for a moment, we are on a winner. We have interrupted the pattern: discomposure = anger.

I was at the station once, waiting for a train that was delayed. The passenger standing by me was particularly agitated. He struck up a conversation, seeking confirmation on his thoughts about the inefficient service. In part, I agreed with him. I had hoped to reduce his tension at least for a while. He asked me if the delay was going to cause problems at work as he has noted that I am not at all upset. I reply that indeed it does, but I guess pointless losing my cool when I can't do anything about it. I suggest he tries the same and he replies: 'It's obviously easy for you, it's your character; you see, I'm not like that' We go our separate ways, clearly he is not comforted, he's actually even more annoyed. Other than being exasperated with the train company, he is annoyed at those people (me) who manage to keep calm under pressure. You see, I didn't start from his operating level, I started from mine.

The tailback

Clive is a manager. He is forty, married and has a young son. Every morning he gets up at half past seven, ready to leave for work at eight-thirty. He goes down to the garage to get his car. At eight thirty-five he is on the road to the office. Everything is planned; he must get there by eight fifty. All goes well for the first five minutes, the traffic is flowing, then it slows to a stop, there are road works ahead. Clive starts emitting clear 'emotional' responses. His jaw contracts, he nervously looks around, he checks the time. Minutes pass and the traffic moves really slowly. Clive becomes increasingly tense. When he finally gets out of the traffic and reaches the office ten minutes late, his tension does not drop, he is now in an optimal situation for becoming aggressive. We call this behaviour displaced aggression and it is directed towards people over which you can exercise power. It rapidly creates a situation of extreme discomfort for all involved. For Clive the unexpected event has ruined his day.

Often we cannot stick to our plans. We organize our day but the unexpected takes us right off course. What can we do? We have done everything we can, but the situation doesn't depend on us, it is useless getting upset. If it does depend on us, getting anxious is a waste of time; we need solutions.

Remember, in seeking solutions we are protagonists and we choose; we must not leave events to decide for us.

Expectations and reading between the lines

We've invited a couple of friends round for dinner at eight-thirty. At eight they call to say their car has broken down and they won't be able to make it, they are stranded out of town. A situation like this probably doesn't bother us. We may feel disappointed, we have prepared a great meal, and we were looking forward to a pleasant evening. We are thinking 'I'm sorry for them, what a hassle! In this way of thinking, we felt sorry for our friends, with perhaps, slight disappointment for the prepared meal. It would be incorrect to think: I cooked dinner and they didn't come, they ruined my evening.

Some of us however, tend to read between the lines. The verbal message: 'We were stuck out of town' might be read as: 'They've made this up, I guess they didn't really want to come' Often we try to interpret behaviour and we hear ourselves commonly thinking in various situations: 'They're snubbing me' or 'It's because he's up-tight about something I've done' or 'It's a payback because I was a bit rude yesterday' or even 'He's not calling obviously because he's not interested'.

The tendency to read between the lines has, as immediate consequence, an increase in aggressiveness. The phrase: 'He's not calling obviously because he's not interested' can have this follow up: 'Since you are not interested in me, I'll act accordingly. I not going to call, I'll see what happens. Let's see what could happen: The friend calls after a few days us and growls: 'It's about time you called, how come it's always me who has to call? It is just too difficult to say 'Nice to hear you, how are you'. Impossible to be nice when our friend has behaved badly (we believe). We need to get used to *NOT READING BETWEEN THE LINES*.

The tendency towards aggressiveness at the missed appointment issue is due to inappropriate thought patterns. Our recurring thought is: 'Everything must go as I want and expect'. When this does not happen we feel we are right to get angry. It is odd that many of us continue to use a non-functional behaviour. What can be useful about getting upset when as sole result we only hurt ourselves? We cannot have friends to dinner when they are unable to come. It would be better to reflect by asking 'How does getting angry serve me and does it solve my problem'? Getting angry in some situations may have its uses, but however, results will only be short-term.

If a friend regularly arrives late for appointments and we are always punctual, we obviously manifest our disappointment. We may receive an apology which provides brief satisfaction, but their behaviour doesn't change, and they will continue to arrive late because their being late has no direct consequences.

A few years back, I used to see a friend two or three times a week. He was regularly twenty or thirty minutes late. I used to get annoyed with him, at which he would apologize and swear to never do it again. Indeed, the result was short-term; he would be punctual for the next two or three times then slips back into his usual pattern. Since getting cross upset only me, I tried other strategies. One of which was also to arrive late. This didn't work either; I didn't like being late and if he got there before me he would point it out, telling me off for having told him off in similar situations! I then pointed out that at least he now knew how irritating it is to be waiting for someone. After all this we ended up quarrelling, almost losing the friendship. But I liked the guy and he was fun to be with, so once again I was the loser, I was paying the higher price. So I worked out another strategy. I explained to my friend that for our next meeting I would wait five minutes, and if he didn't appear, I would move on. I also explained that I really hated hanging around waiting for people. And so it was, the next time I waited five minutes, then left. This way I 'paid' less. This way my friend 'paid' his part of being late; when no-one tuned up at the appointment, his evening was spoiled. To avoid this, he was obliged to be there on time. It worked! He still protests for me doing that but at least he is on time!

Every type of behaviour has its consequences. If there are no negative consequences the behaviour will continue. My friend had continued to arrive late because had I continued waiting for him. As you see I use the past form: Our friendship has not broken up because of my behaviour. We just have fewer occasions to meet up.

Expectations at work

We've started a new job and it's going brilliantly! One year goes by and we expect something new. We know the job well but there is nothing particularly motivating; always the same old stuff. We are getting bored. Boredom, repetitive work, can be a source of anxiety for some. For others, however, repetitive work provides a source of tranquillity; these types get anxious when new things ocour or changes are made. Josh has worked for fifteen years in the bank. At first the work was motivating, he was learning new skills, a lot of things that he hadn't learned while training. Josh learns quickly and asks to be put at the till. But it is repetitive and unstimulating. After a few months he applies for a transfer but he has to wait as the organizational structure does not foresee a new job for him. He is frustrated. His boss tells him he has to hang on for at least another year. It becomes clear that, if you work in an institution (such as banks or public sector), you cannot plan your future. As we have seen, for some this can be comforting, for others a source of anxiety. After fifteen years in the bank, Josh seeks another activity; he starts a small business on his own. Three years have passed; the new job is exciting for Josh, no more boredom, no more anxiety.

Even when we work for ourselves however we cannot implement all our initiatives.

We cannot keep everything under control in given situation. In any case it is better to take action, rather than wait for absolute certainty for success. There is no certainty. If we do not reach a goal that we have set ourselves it is not so important to repeat our actions. So *EVERYTHING IS IMPORTANT BUT NOT SO IMPORTANT.*

Work and creating false expectations: How to lose credibility

I was promised a job that required me to hire a few people. I call my future employees and explain the work to be done. They will start in one month. These are the agreements made with the person who commissioned the work. A month has gone by but red tape issues have prevented us starting the project. This went on for several months. Were told it was only a matter of time (how much time wasn't exactly clear). A year has passed and the work has not been done. I explain to my future collaborators that the delay does not depend on me. In this case I had created expectations to employees; expectations that I have not been able to implement. Let's look at two examples where creating expectations can cause frustration and anger:

1. An employer telling his employees: 'There'll be fantastic incentives at year end'. When the time comes they find fifty euro more in their pay check (yes, *fantastic*). The employees think it is rather a *fantastic* joke. The employer's message is equivocal; he did not say exactly how much the incentive was going to be, thus creating high expectations.

   Take a look at this scheme:

   A) Input of general information.
   B) Expectations are created.

There are two possible developments:

   C1) The information corresponds to the expectations; no problem.
   C2) The information does not correspond to the expectations creating discomfort and frustration. Trust is lost in the person giving unclear information.

2. An employee is guaranteed a promotion. The employer actually states 'You can be sure that in around six months I get you promoted to top manager, you are competent and have the right skills'.
   Here the information is precise. If the promise is kept, all

will be fine. But if in around six months from the employer's assurance of promotion, there is no change in status, the employee will feel duped and highly frustrated.

It may be that sometimes promises can't be kept. In such cases it would be appropriate to communicate such information to all concerned. It will certainly arouse feelings of frustration but not to such a high degree as when no information is given as regards and the promise is not kept.

So, giving hazy information, making promises you can't keep or creating high expectations means losing credibility. It produces malcontent, and consequently obstructive behaviour from all those concerned.

Judgement

There is a tale about the travels of an old man, a boy and a donkey.

As they reach the first village on their journey the people they meet exclaim: 'Look at them, the old man is on foot when he could ride the donkey!' The old man thinks 'They are right' and mounts the donkey.

On reaching the next village he hears the people say: 'Look at the old man, he's riding and the boy has to walk'. They are right' thinks the old man, and pulls the boy up onto the donkey. On reaching his next stop the outraged villagers exclaim: 'Look, two of them riding the poor donkey!'

This is a classic example of how we have to constantly modify our behaviour in order to please others.

Living this way is a source of anxiety. In our communication we seek out signs of approval. It is typical passive behaviour. Aggressive types do not consider other people's opinion. Fear of being judged is tightly bound to a need of approval, which is equally bound to the type of education we received. Typical utterings are 'What will our parents say?' or 'What will our friends say'? 'What will (whoever) say? And so on.

Anybody has the right to judge behaviour. We have to suffer it. Environmental conditioning plays a determining role in shaping a world of values or suppositions to which we constantly refer. We have already seen how we have every right to make requests; and how others have the right to refuse them.

Many find it hard to ask. We hope we will be understood without even talking. Yet it is an arduous task when direct requests are lacking. How come we are unable to make direct requests?

Watch a parent's behaviour, the disapproving glances when the kids make requests. We hear them answer: 'Don't bother me now' or 'It's rude to ask'.

In these phrases the attention is directed towards the 'other' and this direction from us to the other creates 'cognitive distortion'. We develop a thought process which produces constant anxiety. At the moment we are going to make our request we start thinking: 'They can't refuse', 'It would really upset me if I am refused', 'My request isn't such a big deal', it could be a problem for …' Actually, the problem lies with those who cannot make requests. It is not the other person's issue.

Let's try to resolve our problems so we are in a position to help others. For sure we won't be asking advice from someone with a permanently perplexed expression on their face. How can anyone who can't manage their own problems possible help anyone else? Often we use the word 'overreact'. Many of my clients say they do this. We use it to define someone who responds in an exaggerated fashion to events. A friend may judge that behaviour, and they feel even worse; an acquaintance is rude and they spend days worrying in their grievances. It is all about judgement if it is negative we get upset.

So we start asking questions: 'What have I done to deserve that?' Thing is, if you don't start asking questions, you will never have an answer to your own questions. You will be going round in circles to no conclusion. The obvious question: 'What you said really bothered me, can we clear this up?' cannot be asked. We have seen how difficulty in making requests is tightly bound to fear of judgement. But the fear of judgement means we can't say no. 'We were told: 'It's rude to say no; your friend may need a hand, if you refuse what will happen when you need a hand?'

So we don't refuse for fear of losing a friend, partner or other. It is a belief that you can't say no to a friend. Our judgement therefore is:

1) A need for approval.
2) A fear of criticism.

Judgement plays a determining role in all social situations with friends, family, authority, work our partner and in sales circumstances.

Judgement and friends

A good friend asks a favour. We have no desire to do it. We do not know how to say no or find an appropriate excuse. Follow the dialogue between Paolo who is asking a favour to Kevin:

PAOLO: Could you do me a huge favour? My Aunty is arriving today and I'm stuck in the office so I was wondering if you could pick her up at the airport (This is a normal request, but Kevin doesn't want to go, he doesn't like Paolo's aunt and the idea of spending an afternoon with her disturbs him).

KEVIN: I'd be happy to go, but I've got to run some errands with Dad (to avoid negative judgement from Paolo, Kevin invents an excuse. He is incapable of saying what he really thinks).

PAOLO: Don't worry, Aunty is landing at three, you've got plenty of time to go with your Dad because shops don't close till seven-thirty.

KEVIN: Ok then, I'll go (Obviously he'll be feeling irritated with Paolo. Yet Paolo is not at fault, the problem is that Kevin doesn't know how to say no).

Kevin has made two cognitive errors:

1) He thinks refusing a friend is impolite. What would they think of him?
2) He thinks that if Paolo knew him better he wouldn't ask me that kind of favour.

The first error puts Kevin in a passive condition which brings him to make the second error which is thinking his friend can read his mind. Friendship exists when we can speak freely without fear of criticism. Relationships improve when we are able to say no.

You might have passive friends to whom asking favours is difficult; because when they say yes it might mean no. If, for example we choose a movie or where to eat, we decide for ourselves, and this is easy and it saves a lot of time. Often aggressive types choose passive friends, which might be comfortable for both. What I have witnessed is that these types of relationship often don't go the distance. The passive type gets to his limit and becomes aggressive: leaving the decision-making to the other then criticizine the decision taken. You will hear utterances such as 'You wanted to see the film, it was really awful!' Then continue to leave the decision-making to the other. Now, the aggressive type, facing such behaviour may well choose to argue, or even end rapport. From them you will hear: 'It's always me taking decisions and you are always criticising, I'm fed up!' The assertive type will try to reach a compromise. You would hear 'Well, I chose this time, next time is your turn'. However, do not expect to see a rapid change. We are trying to attenuate the criticism following our decision. But it is a waste of time continuing a friendship at such a high price.

We see how judgement is connected to approval and to criticism. Fear of judgement makes us dependent on others and unable to manage criticism. Remember that *WE CAN ONLY JUDGE OUR OWN BEHAVIOUR*. If we are wrong, we pay the consequences. I say this to the passive types. Assertive types consider other's judgement, they assess it, and if it is useful, they accept it. Assertive types therefore are ready to change, not because they want to please someone but because they please themselves. Aggressive types don't even consider other's judgement. Their behaviour, they believe, is right; therefore, they cannot change.

Let's take a peek at another example of difficulty to refuse requests. Silvana has spent the evening with her friend Frank. Frank wants to establish something a little more 'intimate' and is pressing for more. Silvana has no intention of furthering the friendship. When he calls to invite her again, she replies 'I'm really busy this week, I don't have time'. He calls again and Silvana again finds some excuse. Obviously, after a few attempts Frank does not call again. So what was it that stopped Silvana from clearly stating that she had no intention of dating Frank? It was her thought process. Silvana may think: 'If I refuse, he'll think I'm rude.' This way of thinking initially creates discomfort which leads to aggressiveness. Silvana isn't clear; she presumes

Frank understands. Frank however, does not understand, at least, not immediately, and Silvana becomes aggressive. She thinks: 'How can he *not* understand?' When Frank later does realize, he thinks: 'Couldn't she have said straight out instead of inventing a heap of excuses?' Remember, it is our fault if someone doesn't understand.

Judgement and family

Some of my clients have difficulty managing judgement from family members. Here I am talking about negative, guilt-inducing judgement.

One of these, Clara, tells me: 'I decided to get married when I was twenty-two, my parents did not share my decision. My father, as usual, was overtly obstructive. My mother, on the other hand, used to say that they were doing it for my own good. It has always been hard to compete with my mother. I married against their wish. After two years the marriage broke up. My parents judged that equally negatively as by then they had got used to my husband and believed that I was at fault. They also always criticised my job. Eight years after my separation I found a new partner. My parents criticise this relationship too, my partner is twenty years older than me. We've been together for two years and I am happy. He's a nice guy; gentle and understanding. So how can I handle my parents? They accepted my partner, but they keep interfering in my life. For example they insist that every Sunday we go over to theirs. If I tell my father we have other things to do, he makes me feel guilty. He says thing like 'You only think about yourself, and having fun. You don't respect your duties towards the family.

We see two habitual and manipulative behaviours from Clara's parents:

1) Negative judgement or manipulative criticism; easily identifiable when others so not behave as we expect them to.
2) 'Benevolence', that is: 'Do what *I* want for *your* own good'.

Let's see what Clara must learn to be able to handle her parents:

1) How to assess her own emotions when she perceives she is under attack.
2) How to understand and discern which behaviour the parents are using: manipulative or not.
3) How to prepare a competitive response to her parents.
4) How to anticipate her parents' increase in aggressiveness after suitable competitive response.

Clara finds it especially difficult to assess and manage her own emotional responses. Luckily (ironically) her discomfort was not so great, so she could recognize her parents' behaviour. Once we are able to do this we can, successively, use competitive responses. Clara has begun to formulate answers such as: 'I understand you want to see me, but I have already made other arrangements'. When her parents insist, she too insists. At first, her parents became more aggressive; it lasted for a good few months. Then her father, although he still did not share his daughter's views, began to accept her choices and his criticism almost ceased. He still occasionally makes her feel guilty.

The cognitive knowledge of what we have to say is not always enough. This was the case of my fifty-year old lady client. Married with two children, her husband is often away for work. The parents-in-law live in the apartment above. The lady is a passive type. Her mother-in-law often pokes her nose into the lady's life; she often breezes into her daughter-in-law's kitchen and tells her that she must prepare more wholesome food for the family, telling her that the food she makes is not good for men! This obviously creates huge discomfort for my client. It produces an elevated emotional response but she bites her tongue and obeys her mother-in-law wishes. We agree she must become more competitive, so next time the mother-in-law barges in she must learn to say, in a neutral tone, something like: 'Thank you for your advice, however, in my own home I decide what or what not to cook, and what is good and what is bad'. My client agrees and understands that she can decide. We literally practice saying these words with instructions to put to practice at the first occasion. What actually happened was that the intense emotional response made my client unable to remember what it was she should have been be saying.

In this case, my client must first learn how to relax. I teach her how, and then she must visualize the mother-in-law being aggressive. Then we connect relaxing to being under mother-in-law-attack. We do trial runs. I feed in mother-in-law-type criticism while my client practices keeping the emotional response under control. Once she can do this she is ready to produce a competitive response to her mother-in law.

Now her competitive skills have improved; she believes she can have her rights respected and she is having (she guesses) a 50% success rate, she manages to compete when she is directly attacked. Nonetheless, when she is faced with a 'benevolent' manipulation, she tends to give in. However, considering she wasn't able to defend herself is any situation at all; she is now much more confident and decisive. The change process is slow but now she undoubtedly recognizes when she is being passive when suffering manipulation.

Judgement and authority

You are stressed; you've got an exam this morning. You check your notes for the umpteenth time, but it does nothing to reduce a state of pure dread. You are summoned to the exam room. There's no escape. The student before you is still with the examiner and you hear him stumble over a question. The examiner says: 'You don't seem very prepared, let's try another question, if you can't answer this, you'll fail'. Indeed, the student can't answer, so failing the test. You observe examiner's face; he never smiles and is clearly irritated by the student's lack of preparation. It's your turn now and you are seriously flipping out. You sit, spout out some answers and … pass! Will it be so bad next time round? Sadly, yes. If you don't deal with the anxiety and its real cause, it will always be this way, whatever your 'exam' is. Many parents, in the hope of educating their children, are heard to say: 'You've got to give a good impression'. For children and adolescents the parents' judgment counts enormously. Thus we actually learn how to be fretful when trying to give a good impression to the 'authority'.

Those who attach great importance to what others think often behave in two ways. They become aggressive with those of lesser 'authority', tending to belittle and subjugate them or, with those they consider more 'authoritative', they submit and become passive. In these cases the previous statement: *EVERYONE IS IMPORTANT, BUT NOT SO MUCH* holds true. If we accept this statement we will not modify our behaviour according how we perceive 'authority'.

We have considered the relevance of how our parents educate their children however what happens during our school years cannot be ignored. Our teachers bear a huge influence, particularly in the elementary years. If I were to assess a teacher for a job, I would primarily assess their social skills. In business and management it is now a highly considered skill to have today and we often see managers and top managers claiming their position because of their ability to interact and communicate well at a social level. Strange indeed how a teacher's skills in class communication are often ignored, and how a lack of such skills can create considerable tension in the classroom setting where only a few students actually learn and the others are negatively judged. We now know it is our responsibility if someone does not understand because we haven't considered the other's operating level. Starting this way means to understand behaviour, therefore it means understanding that person's skills or lack thereof. On the other hand, negative and positive judgement is always subjective. Using negative judgement is unnecessary, it is useful only to who uses it, because doing so avoids taking responsibility (see chapter on error).

Our culture has taught us to use negative judgement. It is often hard to see the positive aspects in others. We should however, try to do so; it is useful. For example: we negatively judge a work colleague before a meeting. We are edgy and risk becoming aggressive. Here's what happens:

1. A colleague is negatively judged (we have previous experience of their 'bad' behaviour towards us).
2. We meet up with the colleague.
3. We activate negative emotional responses.
4. We tend to avoid or to be aggressive.

Doing this is obviously useless; we *should* be pleasant and friendly. Try to identify something positive or nice or even funny in the person. It will help reduce tension and aggressiveness. There is no double standard in seeking a strategy to calm our nerves to optimize our outcome.

There are no particular authority issues in the case I describe, however we will see that judgement of people we consider important can, similarly, create a permanent state of angst.

Alex is forty-three and a successful businessman. He has made it on his own; his parents were not well off. His role models were all people who had a certain economic bearing. At twenty-five, a skilled manager he was already wealthy. He had been able to emulate people he considered important, but he is not gratified. He wants to prove he is worthy. 'But to whom?' I ask him 'To myself' he replies. The expensive cars, the beautiful women he dates, all go to his wanting to demonstrate the goals he has reached. All this is costing Alex, not economically of course, but in terms of appearance, which he has to maintain. Alex's cognitive errors are:

1) I need to prove my worth.
2) I need to be enviable.

As you see, we never hear the word 'pleasure.' There is nothing wrong with buying a nice car. But we must do it for ourselves, for our pleasure, not for demonstrating status. Therefore, *WE DO NOT HAVE TO PROVE OUR WORTH TO OTHERS.* Nor do we have to prove ourselves. The desire to prove worth is a reflection of someone else's opinion. The individual owning a proper self-assessment uses phrases such as: 'I am satisfied, I like, I don't like'. All statements must be centred on 'self', not on others. Saying: 'I want to prove', is centred on others.

Employees are nearly always under criticism by their superiors. Often the work environment is tense. The desire to excel creates competition between employees. To get ahead you need good ratings. Often the strategy is to disparage a colleague to get in the limelight. Some work situations actually facilitate this system. We find badmouthing in all social groups including family. The question is: 'What purpose does denigrating others to acquire merit serve?' In the short term, it sometimes provides results, long-term it provides nothing. The results will show at short term because they create expectations in the listener. The listener may think this guy sounds pretty confident. But actually what matters are results, which will only be seen in the long term.

This strategy creates expectations in who uses it and who is on the receiving end. The first thinks 'I have to prove my worth', the latter 'Let's see what he is worth'. Often the aggressive type won't even flinch on failing to reach their goal, they have a bloated self-esteem, and the squandered goal, they believe, depends on someone else's incompetence.

Judgement and sales

We go into a store to buy a jacket. We have one of a particular colour in mind. Let's see the dialogue between the customer and the salesperson:

CUSTOMER: I saw a checked jacket last month in the window, the one with side slits.
ASSISTANT: Yes, It was last year's model; they don't do that line anymore. Try this new model; I'm sure it'll look great. (The salesperson expresses negative opinion on the jacket

that the customer wanted, and a positive one on the jacket he wants to sell.)

CUSTOMER: It's not quite what I was looking for, but I'll try it anyway.

ASSISTANT: (Helping the customer put the jacket on, then observing and, showing approval). It fits you nicely; take a look in the mirror. (The assistant continues to show positive feedback. It is a manipulative strategy of the type: 'I know what I'm talking about', insinuating that the customer doesn't like the jacket it is because they know nothing about fashion.)

CUSTOMER: (Although unconvinced). It is a fine jacket. But I'm not comfortable in it (meaning to say he doesn't like it, and seeks an excuse not to buy).

ASSISTANT: That's not a problem. The important thing is that you like it. Where is it not comfortable?

CUSTOMER: On the back and around the sleeves. It is not a good fit. (He keeps making excuses. It may be true that the jacket is slightly tight, but he still does not say that he doesn't like the jacket).

ASSISTANT: 'No bother. I'll call the tailor. We'll get this fixed.'

At this point the customer is forced to buy the jacket. Let's see the cognitive errors:

a. The salesperson's opinion is more important than mine;
   b. I mustn't show that I'm inept.
c. The salesperson very kind, I don't want to waste his time and not buy anything.

In this case, the cognitive 'distortion' does not allow him to achieve the goal he set for himself i.e. to buy the jacket he wanted, and if not in this store, in another. At behaviour level the error is to have bought the jacket he didn't want. Remember it is the manifest behaviour that is important. We all have cognitive distortions at some level or the other. What matters is achieving the goal we have set ourselves. In the case of the store, *we* have to be satisfied, not the salesperson. When we reach a goal, however small, we feel gratified. Reaching success in self-affirmation enables us to be more confident in future situations. The customer leaves the shop, having bought the jacket that he did not want, he feels frustrated. He thinks, 'I am totally incapable if imposing myself, unable to say what it is I want'. Thus confirming the inability to handle even simple situations and having a low opinion of self. Managing sales situations is not particularly difficult because there is little emotional involvement. In these situations, keep sight of the goal is fundamental. In the above case, the customer could have behaved as follows:

1)   Try the jacket on.
2)   Decide if he liked it or not.

If he didn't, an assertive response could be: 'It is a nice jacket, but it's not what I want.' If the salesperson insists we say: 'I understand, but it is not what I wanted, thank you'. We use the 'stuck record' technique, which is, repeating calmly the same words without getting involved in any further line of patter.

Judgement and partner

Take a situation when judging our partner activates an intense emotional response. Laura and her husband are at a dinner with three other couples. There is discussion on the latest political developments, everyone expresses their opinion. Laura gives hers, her husband, with one look declares his total disapproval. Laura is instantly edgy and doesn't utter another word for the rest of the evening. Feeling of constantly judged and observed creates endless tension. Why do partners often make negative judgments? Mainly for two reasons:

1) They don't want their companion to give a 'bad impression' (I don't want others to judge negatively).
2) They believe their partner can't handle certain situations without their guidance (we read: they must behave as I wish).

If we accept the statement: 'Nobody has the right to judge', we must be able to not judge. Remember, assertiveness is: 'I'm fine with that person'; 'I'm not fine with ...'; 'I like or I do not like'.

The phrase: 'So and so is unpleasant' is aggressive. We can only say: 'I'm uncomfortable with that person'; do not generalize. That person may be unpleasant for me, but pleasant for someone else. So *WE DO NOT CRITICIZE OTHERS*. We have already seen how, the essence of friendship is being able to liberally express yourself. This also applies to our relationships. We must be able to express ourselves freely, if that does not appeal to our partners, then it must be discussed. In discussion, we accept helpful criticism but disregard manipulative criticism.

One of my clients describes his wife as 'unbearable.' When they are together, she takes over the conversation. She criticizes him in front of all and sundry. Since this was his version of things, I decide to see them together. The wife begins talking; I interrupt to hear what the husband has to say. She butts in before he has the chance to speak. She is openly aggressive towards her husband; she is over-confident and knows what she wants. She says she is the decider and declares her husband is unable to do so. She states this quite clearly in front of him.

At the next session I see my client alone. He reiterates the fact that his wife has an awful character. He is hoping I agree to his negative judgement. But to what use? Well actually, none at all. He is the hen-pecked husband. He needs to learn to manage his discomfort. When the wife attacks him, he feels physically sick. It is clear that ranting on about his wife's character is a waste of time, since she has no intention of changing; for she is doing just fine as she is. Once he accepts that his wife will not change, he has two choices at hand to alleviate discomfort, where following the first rules out the second: do what you can to manage your distress at aggressiveness, or, if unsuccessful, consider separation (second strategy). Now, two years later, my client is fine. He left his wife a year and a half ago.

Judgement and society

It is often said that in life it is important to have the values you believe in. It is very difficult to know *which* values. Everybody is different and each has their own values. Here's my first objection to the affirmation 'There are universally accepted values.' If you agree with this it will be difficult to accept a different viewpoint. Think about what's important to you, it may be the concept of friendship, family, religion or nation and so on.

It's easy to find a value you believe in and so far, so good. But when the value takes on an inordinate significance for us, we begin to get stuck in standing our ground, we find it hard to accept when someone thinks and acts differently. So prejudice arises and the establishment of groups which discard those who are different. These types know, and are sure about what is good and what is bad. The value they believe in becomes absolute, only they can judge. Of course most of us are not so extreme or absolute, but if we take a close look at ourselves, we will discover that too often we are intolerant towards those who live differently from us. If we value the family and then witness the wife of a friend leaving her husband, we condemn. Why do we negatively judge someone who has never criticized us? Although no direct confrontation has occurred we feel that our values have been violated. Therefore we justify our blaming of the different behaviour. Observe the following scheme:

1) Situation in which a person emits a behaviour.
2) The output behaviour is not acceptable and is contrary to our universe of values.
3) It disturbs us, we feel uncomfortable.
4) We have to ward off the discomfort.
5) We become aggressive, we condemn.
6) The discomfort ceases, we are satisfied with our behaviour, we were right.

We see how 3 created discomfort followed by 4, avoidance. We attach *our* discomfort to the other's behaviour. It is the other who has done wrong. It is right to 'condemn'. We have seen, in the chapter on expectations how we blame the other for our discomfort and we want others to modify accordingly. We might realize that we have to change ourselves, we have been uncomfortable for too long. But the 'absolute thinker' does not change. The discomfort is momentary; the aggressive response (negative judgment) is immediate.

If we believe it is essential for our own wellbeing to be able to communicate with everyone, we have to free ourselves from prejudice, understand different points of view and identify the suppositions that prevent acceptance of others. One way is to seek common ground on which to establish a relationship. In later chapters we will use dialogues that aim to dismantle some suppositions that make us rigidly hold a position and thwart our understanding of others.

Judgement and perfection

Maria is twenty-five; she is an employee in a large industry. Endowed with good social skills and speaks three languages.

She often refuses tasks which consider her specific skill set. She is afraid to expose herself and claims she is unsuitable for the task. On observation, her speech is precise and she comments only when it she is confident of what she is saying; she is always affable and kind, elegantly dressed and graceful in manner. These are positive qualities, so what keeps her from emerging? She also declares she is not particularly satisfied with her current job. We analyse a dialogue between Maria and her friend, Mark:

MARIA: I'd like to change jobs, find something better paid and more rewarding.

MARK: Have you got any ideas? You've been telling me this for over a year.

MARIA: It's true, I know, I'm just not satisfied with the job.

MARK. What exactly isn't satisfying?

MARIA: I don't seem to be able to move forward and it's boring and tedious.

MARK: You said you always pass up when they ask you to do something different.

MARIA: I know. I'm so afraid I'm not up to the task.

MARK: Ok, but surely you have to put yourself out there if you

want to change? Anyway what sort of job are you looking for?
MARIA: I really don't know.
MARK: You've got loads of skills; you could look out something
    along those lines.

Six months have gone by since this conversation, and Maria is still in the same job. She'll probably be there for years to come. Maybe she regrets her choice and has misgivings for what she could have done. The fear of being judged by others, linked to the self-image she needs to create, prevents her from shifting operating level. Talking about what we *could* do is useful only when we have switched operating level; that is, if you are already moving in that direction. In Maria's case, she should prove herself in the job she already has, to assess her real skills, learn how to accept criticism and from her mistakes. Being perfect is not a skill; there is a certain skill however in resisting the frustration that being unsuccessful creates.

Assessing judgement

I asked thirty of my clients (twenty women and ten men) with social anxiety to give a rating, in order of importance for the following relationship types: friends, family, authority, partner, and sales.

Twenty-five gave family and partner at first place followed by friend, authority and sales situations.

Four gave a similar response but placed authority before friends.

One client gave the following: authority, sales, friends, family and partner in last place. On investigation of the reasoning behind their choices, twenty nine of them gave the same answer. Most important were family and partner: we live together. Friends can change, here today, gone tomorrow. The authority figure may cause discomfort, but we don't have to live together. Sales situations were least important.

The four clients who put authority first were all employees, and suffered discomfort around their superiors. The only client whose order of importance was completely inverted was a twenty-three year old university student. He gets full marks for his studies. He tells me he wants to shine in life. His reasoning for placing authority first was significant. He reasoned that he needed the judgement of the authority figure to get ahead in life. 'These people can help me', he states. For him, on the other hand, the sales situation often brought discomfort; he explained they were often difficult to handle. Friends however, sometimes could be useful. He placed his mother, grandmother (his father died a few years ago) and girlfriend in last place. Regarding his mother, he feels she will never judge him, whatever he does and she won't abandon him. His grandma is old and there is no dialogue. His girlfriend accepts him just as he is.

In all thirty assessments for judgement, we find that the order is given depending on the importance each person has for us. There is no right classification. All twenty-nine similar assessments have issues with family (particularly their parents), partner or authority. They tend to passivity. As for the young student, his constant need to distinguish himself has brought him to physical exhaustion to the point where he is unable to sit exams.

It is essential not to feel discomfort. Nearly all of my clients need to learn how to handle their family or other relationships. The student, on the other hand, needs to understand that trying to be number one all the time can be very costly.

Once we have recognized the judgement or criticism that disturbs us we can prepare the response, or better, a counter-step for each one. It would be opportune:
1) To identify the criticisms to which you are most vulnerable.
2) To write them down in a list.
3) To prepare, for each one, a light-hearted counter-response.

This way we don't need to be aggressive or suffer those who criticize, and it will for sure puts an end to any further aggression towards us. Often after enduring criticism we wonder what it was we *could* have said. So, to move on from just thinking 'good intentions', to making a real change, we have to prepare adequate replies, and these must become automatic. For example to: 'You are putting on weight!' The answer could be: 'I love food.'

Willpower

Willpower doesn't exist. Hard to believe isn't it? What exactly do we mean by willpower? Often we hear phrases like: 'I just haven't got it in me. I'm made that way'. All useless utterances meaning nothing and that certainly won't help us change. These thoughts are demotivating and passive in form. People spend thousands of hours studying or playing music, some climb mountains and dedicate days on end to do so; others spend weeks programming a PC. Is that just because they have willpower?

If you ask how they do it, they will probably reply: 'I just love doing it'.

A stimulus to self-development is accepting the difficulties we may encounter, endure suffering or disappointment; there are people who have learned to live with that. We tend to engage in activities that gratify us and give results, both short and long term. We can demonstrate 'will' in one area but not in another. The climber who is committed for hours on a difficult wall may not be able to do repetitive work; they are soon bored to tears and highly unmotivated. Therefore *DO NOT INCRIMI-NATE SELF OR OTHERS FOR LACK OF WILLPOWER.*

Willpower and work

Remember our friend Josh, the disgruntled banker? I occasionally see his wife. She tells me that when they married, Josh had been working in the bank for three years and he was already dissatisfied with the job. When I ask her if he had ever considered changing jobs, she observes 'All his colleagues seem happy and it's a safe and easy job, and if Josh were more determined, he would accept it. There are so many things in life that we don't want to do, but you just have to get on with it'.

This is a classic, and we can re-write it like so: 'Will is doing what we *have to* do, not what we *want* to do; doing what we like doing is not willpower'. But what we *have to* do is to self-gratify or gratify someone else. Often we don't do things for ourselves, but for someone else's wellbeing.

Josh had huge issues entertaining the idea of changing jobs as he met up against two hurdles:

1) His wife's inability to understand why he should give up the security of employment for a less secure work.
2) How Josh's parents saw a job in the bank meant having a good social standing.

Both wife and parents attributed Josh with scarse will and adaptability. If Josh had changed his job, both parents and wife would fret. Therefore for their peace of mind he had carried on the job in the bank. He managed to break away only fifteen years later.

Willpower and controlling behaviour

Carla weighs one hundred and five kilos. She has tried many diets, but with no consistent results. She lost thirty kilos in two months, and put it all back on in in two. She is thirty-five, married with two children. She runs a shop and employs an assistant. The husband is often away on business. Carla has been overweight since childhood, but not much above the average. Only eight years ago she began to gain more, and four years ago, reached her current weight. She is determined to slim down. I advise her to keep a detailed diary, and write down everything she eats, with particular attention to the food she consumes between meals. I see Carla after eight days. She had kept the diary scrupulously. She noted: time of eating, amount of food, anxiety she felt at that moment, any events preceding eating. I wanted to test the following hypotheses:

1) If there were any anxiety-producing events prior to eating.
2) If there was a positive correlation between level of anxiety (assessed subjectively) and food intake.

First hypothesis: We identified anxiety-producing events; Carla is not able to handle her relationship with the in-laws, husband and mother. She is passive-aggressive with all of them. When she issues inappropriate behaviour in an interpersonal situation, she suffers anxiety for several days on end.

Second hypothesis: When Carla's anxiety is high, she eats more often. On her worse days she can get from eight to ten snacks between meals. Her favourite foods are sweet. So the answer to the second hypothesis is 'yes', there is correlation between anxiety and food.

When she eats excessively, she feels guilty. Unable to control herself, she says: 'I'll never lose weight.' therefore she tends towards depression, and her anxiety increases. This vicious circle can be seen as:

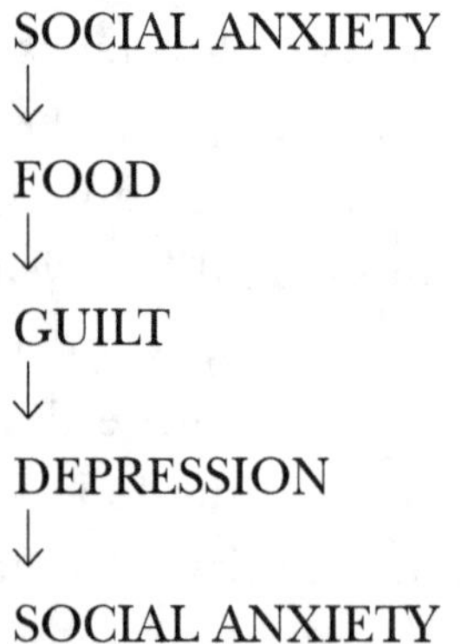

In this case we can't say that the lack of will is the cause of overeating. If the suppositions we have made are correct, acquiring social skills should reduce Carla's anxiety levels and thus food intake. In many obese people you can identify social situations that facilitate an increase of food intake. In Carla's case we need to teach her how to manage social anxiety, although acquiring social skills may not be enough. She has now created a tight link between the sight of food and food response. Attention is centred on controlling the food stimulus. Carla must remove food from her sight. For example, remove the nearby chocolates when watching TV. Only when the link 'sight of food = feed' is broken, will Carla be able to lose weight.

Often our responses to certain situations are disproportionate. We are aware of the futility of these responses. They tell us that with a little 'will' we be able to gain control, but it is an arduous task. After issuing the inappropriate behaviour, we try to justify it. We hear phrases such as: 'He made me angry. He shouldn't have done that, of course I get angry'. Let's change these sentences, because they are detrimental said this way. Therefore, let's *NOT JUSTIFY OUR OWN BEHAVIOUR.*

Non-control of emotional responses, together with justification, maintains behaviour.

Therefore, we cannot talk about non-willpower in self-control, rather, a self-control 'disability'. Our inappropriate behaviour can be described as follows:

STIMULUS EVENT
↓
EMOTIONAL RESPONSE
↓
INAPPROPRIATE BEHAVIOUR
↓
SELF-JUSTIFICATION OF
↓
INAPPROPRIATE BEHAVIOUR

Self-justification of our behaviour does not allow us to change it; therefore the probability of emitting the same behaviour in a similar situation increases. We can try to change the self-justifying phrases:

1) 'He/she made me angry.' I got angry so we must say: 'I am angry'.
2) 'He/she shouldn't have done that'. Remember we do not expect others to behave in any way, I got upset, and so what can I do not to be upset? How should I change my behaviour?
3) 'Of course I am angry'. Since it is a waste of time getting angry, you should say: 'If a similar situation occurs again I'll not get angry.'

The blaming brother

If we want to change our behaviour we have to change the way we think.

Look at the poor communication between two brothers, Andy and Simon:

ANDY: What were you doing at mum's yesterday? You hardly ever go. *I* see her at least two or three times a week. She's getting on and only has me to count on. (He is being clearly aggressive and uses blame).

SIMON: (Andy makes him ill at ease; he gives emotional responses and also tries to make his brother see reason.) 'I pop in when I think she needs me. It's not easy to be there more often. You know mum, she's always complaining about some ailment or other. She's had all the necessary check-ups but for her age, she's actually doing fine, it's just that when I go she spends hours ranting about her problems and when I finally leave, I'm upset. (Simon communicates the reason of his rare visits to his mother and 'expects' that Andy understands.)

ANDY: It's easy for you; that puts all the responsibility on me (Andy continues aggressively blaming Simon)

SIMON: (Trying to reason with his brother doesn't work, he is getting up tight and his expectation that Andy will understand modifies to 'he doesn't want to understand') 'Maybe you've forgotten about your accident, they rushed you to hospital, I found the best doctors, and I got you transferred to a private clinic to get the best care possible. And if you remember I paid for everything, as you said you couldn't afford it. Now just you come and tell me that I'm not interested! When you've needed me, I have always been there.

(Simon reacted by attacking his brother, blaming him, hoping to reduce Andy's aggressiveness).

ANDY: Fine! So you remind me of that. Who helped find you a job? If it wasn't for me and the people I know, you wouldn't have got anywhere. (Both brothers are digging up the past, here is another manipulative strategy, remembering who did what for whom. We will go into this in the chapter on 'Sacrifice').

SIMON: Since you are not being reasonable, I'm going.

Let's look at this from Simon's point of view:

Question: Does his brother's behaviour upset Simon?
Answer: Yes, it does.
Question: Has he ever been able to change his brother?
Answer: No, Never!

Therefore: Why does Simon continue doing the same thing and get no result?

Take a look below:

1) Stimulus event: Andy attacks.
2) Simon's emotional response.
3) Simon tries to reason with Andy.
4) Andy does not understand (for Simon, Andy doesn't *want* to understand).
5) Simon attacks Andy.
6) Simon as consequence is upset.
7) Simon justifies his behaviour.

Here we can see some of Simon's cognitive errors.

1) Simon's attention is towards the stimulus situation: Andy's

attack. Given that this upsets him (emotional response), he wants to modify it. But Andy has never changed a thing. (See previous questions).

2) Simon's wants his brother to understand his reasoning, even if Andy takes no notice. He persists in his own behaviour because he believes Andy's understanding is only a question of him *wanting to*. The conclusion is now obvious: Simon shouldn't want to convince his brother as it is impossible. He mustn't focus attention on Andy's aggressive behaviour.

Let's see how Simon could have behaved:

ANDY: Why did you go did you go to mum's yesterday? (Aggression and blame).

SIMON: (No provocation accepted) Thank you for looking after her so well.

ANDY: Yes, but seeing as she is also *your* mother, you could show a bit more interest (Continued aggression).

SIMON: (Does not accept aggression and does not justify his own behaviour). I understand you worry about mum, but please don't expect that I do the same (and ends conversation).

Thus Simon is not aggressive (a behaviour that upsets him), more importantly, he doesn't suffer. When Simon is alone he can think: 'I understand that Andy has issues with mum, and I'm sorry. *This is his problem, not mine.*' Obviously this affirmation is clearly different if we compare to the self-justification that would have followed his aggressive behaviour, which would have been: 'He makes me furious every time, he doesn't see my reasoning, he is impossible'.

An affirmation of this kind means Simon doesn't have to change in any way at all.

Pride

We have already seen how expectation contains an excessive self-assessment, and how this prevents us from achieving our aims. Pride can also be defined as an excess of self-assessment. Proud people expect that others assess them in the same way they do for themselves. Proudness ascribes 'importance', and, therefore, *is* important. Others are worth less, obviously. The 'other' owes us consideration and must approve what we say. 'Others must, while we owe 'nothing'.

Starting on the wrong foot

Andy has a dinner date with Francesca. They like each other from the start. They are both outgoing and get on well. Dinner ended, they decide to meet again. Andy knows Francesca is free the next evening, he has no ties, and would really like to see her again. However, he makes a date for the week after. Why does he do this? It seems weird to be so keen to see someone, know that it is feasible and yet postpone the date. Andy reflects: 'I really like Francesca, but I don't want to look too keen, I lose my advantage. She said she likes me, but I don't want to come over like I'm too available, if I'm too available, I'll be less interesting'.

So they meet for dinner, and then go to Francesca's. They spend a wonderful evening and end up a great match in bed. Francesca is outgoing with many interests and friends. She takes things as they come, without asking too many questions or creating too many doubts. Andy tends to 'manage' his relationships and believes it is good strategy to create a sort of 'something to look forward to' situation. As Andy leaves he says 'I'll call you soon, maybe next week, I'm pretty busy right now'. 'Great!' - Francesca replies – 'Call me when you are free, It'll be nice to catch up, I've had a great evening, just let me know in time so I can get sorted'.

Francesca is used to being independent, if Andy rings, great, but it's not a problem if he doesn't, life goes on as ever.

Andy, on the other hand, is saying: 'Now I've really got to be cool, I'll wait to call her, just to check how interested she really is'.

Andy, thinking he is handling it, by not showing up too enamoured, holds off calling her, but in doing so is unhappy.

Francesca, in the meantime, gets on with her life.

This is not excessive assessment in Andy's case, rather a common cognitive error, which is the idea that it's uncool to state your feelings. Therefore you don't say: 'I love being around you' or 'I like you' or 'I care for you'. Many of my clients tell me they find these things compromising; to exposing. Is this way of thinking useful? What is the positive outcome? If we do something, we do it to obtain something else, even if that doing is aimed at momentarily reducing our discomfort. The classic example is how we avoid those who criticize us. Avoidance keeps the discomfort at bay, but it doesn't teach us how to resolve the disturbing situation to our advantage.

We don't use compromising words because often we fear refusal, or non-acceptance, and tell ourselves 'I'm too proud to accept refusal'.

Take a look below:

1) Situation: we like someone.
2) Need to show interest.
3) Afraid of rejection.
4) Find justification: don't want to compromise myself.
5) Avoid showing interest.
6) Say we are too proud.
7) Miss our goal of hanging out with someone we like.
8) New justification; we didn't like them anyway: 'I'm not interested, I got it wrong'.

So even when we don't reach our objectives, self-justification means we don't see our unsuccessfulness, and therefore avoid discomfort.

Pride and work

Let's take a look at Andrea. He's a representative; he started this job around a year ago. The company he works for gave him a client portfolio and expects a minimum turnover. After one year he has lost clients and is below the minimum sales. Obviously, he gets the sack! To understand what happened let's take a look at the dialogue between Andrea and his friend Mark.

ANDREA: Did I tell you they sacked me from the job?

MARK: What happened, it was a good job, I'm really sorry.

ANDREA: This kind of work means working with some really unbearable and arrogant people. Some are so unpleasant to us reps.

MARK: I understand, but your job was to sell, you don't have to worry about whether they've got good manners!

ANDREA: Easy to say, but if you've got any dignity, you can't accept that king of treatment. Just because they are spending money doesn't mean they have to be rude.

MARK: You'll have lost a lot of customers then, probably also the big spenders.

ANDREA: I'm not getting you, you'd have just stood in front of them and put up with their rudeness, No, I can't accept it, if a customer is rude, I don't call again.

MARK: Yes, I would have just focussed on the sale. That would be my gratification, much worse to leave and not get the sale.

ANDREA: Where is your self-respect? You have no dignity!

MARK: I don't care about self-respect, if it prevents me from reaching my goals.

In this case Andrea's pride prevents him from reaching his objectives at work. How can we modify this type of thinking? We must focus on our goals. Other's behaviour must not interfere with us reaching them. In Andrea's case, the customer's rudeness is irrelevant if he wants to prove his worth, which he can only do by selling.

Often we use the word 'pride' to mask a lack in skill. Let's look at a simple reasoning for when we want to reach a goal.

Question: do you think you have the necessary skills?

If yes:

1) Demonstrate them by reaching goals.
2) I thought I was able to reach my goals, I failed. Therefore I
   ask:
— Where did I go wrong and what skills are lacking?
— Can I learn the skills I need?
— If yes, how much time do I need to acquire them?
— Who can I ask to help me or who can I get to do the things
   that I'm not able to.

If not:

3) I don't think I can: modify the goal.
4) I want to give it a try: ask questions in point 2.

Remember *ONLY ASK QUESTIONS TO WHICH YOU CAN GIVE AN ANSWER.*

It is easier to twist reasoning in doubt and uncertainty than it is to think in a simple, linear and operative fashion. This is why it is easier to get upset.

Pride and error

Many of us do not recognize our own mistakes. We make mistakes at work but blame it our colleagues. Marriages end when we decide it is our partner who doesn't understand. We have little rapport with our children because nowadays 'They don't respect us as parents'. The proud person cannot recognise their mistakes because it would ruin self-image. These types have no self-deprecation; they don't know how to capture the negative, yet humoristic side of their behaviour. Taking yourself too seriously, unable to 'take the mickey' leaves you vulnerable.

If, for example, we are at ease and have a laugh in telling friends how awkward and clumsy we were in a certain situation we are obviously not vulnerable to criticism as we are completely in agreement with whoever may offer criticism. So how do those who try to hide their negative side behave?

Their thought pattern is something like:

— I know I feel uncomfortable in that situation.
— I can't accept felling this way, nor can I let it show.
— I must appear cool and casual.
— But will I be able to keep myself in check? In any case I must make a good impression.

These very thoughts will create further discomfort, which leads to withdrawing. The 'proud' type, needing to create a good impression, will not unmask and therefore, will not learn.

So what, exactly, does 'negative side', mean? We reckon that negative is only 'violence', which is, behaving aggressively to others, imposing our points of view. So what is negative about admitting we are afraid or anxious in certain situations, or not knowing how to manage rapport? Can it ever be useful to leave our weaknesses or errors unclaimed?

We 'do' things because we expect some sort of result. By not admitting our mistakes we keep our self-image intact, this is gratifying. Beware; this becomes a vicious circle and tough to get out of. Remember, the proud over-assess themselves, they tend to want to emerge from what they consider 'the masses' and to reach this aim, slander others. The rule is: *DO NOT DENIGRATE OTHERS TO YOUR ADVANTAGE.*

Error

'Be careful! Don't mess up! Behave!' These and other similar phrases we often hear and, even more often, say. We usually mean well, not wanting our children, relatives or friends to make mistakes. We have made our mistakes so we know what is good and what is wrong. Unfortunately projecting this onto others is a huge mistake. This is our experience and as such means we start from our operating level. We had a bad experience which we were unable to handle, but this doesn't mean that others are unable to overcome difficulties that for us seem insurmountable. We have no right to say 'I know what is right or wrong for you'. We can only think 'I know what is right or wrong for me'.

Often we try to prevent others from making mistakes to reduce our own levels of anxiety. We prevent our children from going through a certain experience in the fear that something dreadful will happen. It reduces our anxiety and we feel better. Obviously, we raise objections:

1) My kids must keep good company, I don't want them ending up drug addicts.
2) I must make sure my kids don't do dangerous things, like riding motorcycles.
3) I must plan their future.
4) It's it good to worry about them.

I use examples to reply to these objections. Let's look at two young girls' behaviour and their parents' education style.

Error and parents

The girls, Elena and Marina, are both seven years old; they are both bright and do well at school. Right now Elena is climbing a tree, while her father watches. At about one metre up she calls out that she is afraid. Her father calms her down and encourages her to continue, explaining the best way to climb the tree and teaching her how to overcome discomfort and fear. This parent is not apprehensive, he reassures his daughter, giving security and teaching a skill. Elena is learning how to overcome her fear and when she feels discomfort is able to tell herself: 'Keep calm and think about what I'm doing'. It is necessary to highlight the importance of an 'inner voice'; what we tell ourselves is fundamental to the way we feel, it can reassure or increase our anxiety. Elena is developing her 'inner voice' which will allow her to control her emotions, thus allowing her to reach her desired objectives. To better understand take a look at the scheme below:

1) Adverse situation.
2) Emotional response (tension, high heart rate).

3) Cognitive response: Check myself and find a solution.
4) Motor response: move towards goal.

The father's intervention is in points 2 and 3. At 2: the father's mere presence, calm and collected will inhibit Elena's negative emotional response. Moreover, his reassuring voice reduces her anxiety. At 3: Elena carries out the father's encouragement.

The second girl, Marina, lives with her grandparents. The mother, a widow, is often away for work. Marina is in the living room with her grandparents and is climbing up onto the back of the sofa. Grandma is on the spot: 'Careful, you'll fall'; and lifts her down from the sofa. Now we see Marina playing with her friends. They go up and down a slide of around two metres high, they are more or less her same age. Marina is fearful, but with her friends around, she wants to try. As soon as she reaches the ladder, Grandma butts in and stops Marina from climbing up. Marina protests to no avail; Grandma is firm; Marina is not going on the slide. Successively Grandma hardly ever takes her to play with the other kids. Take a look at the scheme:

1) Marina is about to climb the slide.
2) Grandma feels the situation is dangerous.
3) Grandma emits emotional responses (anxiety).
4) Grandma stops Marina and makes her get down.
5) Grandma is less anxious.
6) Grandma doesn't want to end up in adverse situations (for herself) therefore doesn't take Marina to play with the other kids.

This style of education will train children to be anxious, unable to compete with their own emotional responses. This type of child will tend to avoid situations before they even happen, and thus will never know if they are able to overcome them.

Error and significant other

The fear of failure can in hi bit behaviour. This type of fear is closely related to fear of judgment, a topic that we have already discussed. The husband has to go to a meeting he considers important. He talks to his wife in the days leading up to the meeting and spells out his uncertainties and doubts. He has to take the floor, speaking in front of twenty people and support their points of view. He has never done anything similar, he is afraid of making mistakes and not being able to express himself clearly. We observe the conversation:

HUSBAND: I don't know if I'll be able to express myself proper-
ly, I'm sure I'm going to mess it up.
WIFE: How can you know if you've never tried?
HUSBAND: It's exactly because I've never done it before, it
scares me.
WIFE: So what are you afraid of?
HUSBAND: 'Making mistakes, not being coherent.
WIFE: In any case you have to go; you told me that you have to.
HUSBAND: I know I have to go, we'll also be discussing my busi-
ness interests.
WIFE: I don't think you have to demonstrate your speaking skill,
that's not the point. You know what you have to say and you
are more prepared than others, aren't you?
HUSBAND: Yes. I'm well prepared and I know the subject better.
WIFE: If they raise issues are you ready to answer them?
HUSBAND: I think I can, even I'm not feeling easy about it.

WIFE: So don't worry, you know your job, you know the topic and you can counter-attack any issues that crop up.

In almost all the other situations, we have seen how the partners' actions are destructive. In this case, the wife urges her husband to expose himself. So when, exactly can we push a person to expose themselves?

1) When you possess the skills necessary to deal with the situation, but anxiety (emotional response) blocks output.
2) When we have already dealt with that type of anxiety under similar circumstances.

In this case, the wife correctly assesses her husband, knowing that he possesses the skills necessary to deal with the situation; the only obstacle is his fear of judgment which prevents him from exposing himself. It is obvious that his wife is not worried that her husband might mess up, as she would be the first to advise him against doing the presentation.

It is the husband who predicts a negative performance, which serves no purpose; it only activates our negative emotional responses and impacts on the future performance. We must focus attention on what we have to *do*, not on the thoughts we have about the *doing*. Therefore *DO NOT PROPHESISE NEGATIVE OUTCOME.*

The teacher and error

The teachers are at a school meeting, the maths teacher complains to his colleagues about the poor results in class. He says that only five out of thirty pupils have pass marks. His colleagues are surprised; they have better results with the same class. If we observe the maths teacher during the lesson we can understand what's going on.

He is explaining the lesson whilst writing quickly on the blackboard. Once done and without even looking at the class he exclaims: 'That's all clear, isn't it?' Then he rubs the board clean. For sure it is clear to the teacher, but what about the pupils? If a pupil asks for explanations he repeats the same thing at the same speed with the same words. He then asks a student if he has understood. The student, having understood nothing replies 'Sure'. It's like those awful moments when we go abroad; we try to speak in a foreign language even though our knowledge of the language is limited. We ask, let's say, for directions, receive a rapid and incomprehensible reply, explain that we did not understand, and the whole answer is repeated at the same speed with the same words. So we grin inanely, nod our heads, but haven't understood a single word.

In both cases the teacher and the native speaker do not start from the operating level of those they are talking to.

So how should the teacher behave?

1) By identifying the student's actual level of knowledge of the subject.
2) By planning lessons and exercises staring from the students effective level of knowledge.
3) By understanding the student's difficulty and modify the lesson plan accordingly.

The teacher's constant attention to information on the student's learning means he can adjusts to the level of student's learning.

Clearly this teacher must constantly revisit his style of teaching, accept student's criticism, or better still, ask for their feedback.

Now our maths teacher has called the student to the front and asks a question. The student writes on the board with the teacher hovering nearby, ready to pounce on the first mistake. The student hesitates, and the maths teacher presses him, with words such as 'Come on, it's easy, if you can't do this part, imagine what'll happen when it gets more difficult'. Obviously the student starts giving emotional responses, and if before he knew in part what he had to do, now he shows that he knows nothing. At the end of the interrogation both teacher and student are exhausted. The teacher is tense in trying to spot the mistakes, and when he does he becomes angry and so does the student because he is under constant pressure. The teacher has declared that his class are slow learners, but it is unlikely that he will ever admit that it is he, not the students to err.

Discomfort and drugs

An eighteen year old is going to a party. He spots a girl he likes and strikes up conversation although he feels rather awkward. He needs get the feeling under control. He drinks some whisky, and after the second one he is feeling more comfortable and sure of himself. The teenager actually possesses good social skills but they emerge only when he feels comfortable in his surroundings. Now he can control the situation and talk to the girl with confidence. So what has he learned? That drinking rapidly reduces his awkwardness and discomfort.

What has he not learned? He has not learned how to keep his emotional responses in check. He is not seeing that if he can 'do it', it means he does have the skills, therefore, he can 'do it' without having to drink.

The same mechanism applies for use of tranquillizers: A student feeling anxious prior to exams drops a pill and passes the exam. The same thing occurs at work; when the going gets tough, drop a pill and handle the situation better. If our daily life presents several anxiety producing scenarios, there will be several occasions to take tranquillizers.

So we've seen how using drugs will reduce discomfort and maximize performance. However, this is not always the case. There are times when taking drugs will actually produce a negative performance. In such cases, after performance failure, depression sets in, requiring further use of drugs.

Let's look at the various scenarios:

1) A situation similar to something we have successfully overcome, but always felt anxious prior to performance. An example is the anxiety we feel before exams.
2) A situation similar to something we have not been able to overcome. For example knowing we should speak out at work meetings but always avoid doing so.
3) A new untested situation; one we do not yet know if we are able to handle.

In the first case, we have the skills to cope, but regardless, feel anxiety prior to tackling the situation.

In the second, we do not know if we have the necessary skills because we have always avoided the situation.

In the third situation, seeing as we are facing something new, we simply feel anxious.

Therefore we may or may not have the skills to tackle a situation. In certain circumstances, there are three types of response:
1) A cognitive response, that is, our way of thinking.

2) An emotional response, such as increase in muscle tension, perspiration or palpitations.
3) A motor response, the ones plainly observable.

If we possess the required skills, yet anxiety prevails we may witness the following behaviour sequence:

1) Negative thoughts before facing the situation.
2) Activation of emotional response.
3) Use drugs to reduce anxiety.
4) Momentary reduction of anxiety.
5) Ability to face the situation and obtain positive outcome.

In this sequence we have learned to use tranquilizers every time we face an awkward situation. But we *haven't* learned or modified our cognitive or emotional responses.

We have created a vicious whit a clear link where discomfort = tranquilizers.

If we have no skills, for sure the drug cannot provide them.

Let's imagine a simple task such as driving the car. At first we are worried, excited and afraid, but the more we practice, the more we are able to master the skill so our fear decreases.

Obviously, facing the numerous daily situations is more complex than driving a car. But if we remind ourselves that the more skills we acquire, the less uncomfortable we will feel.

The skill is how to face difficulty, not how to avoid it.

Possessiveness

Possessiveness and jealousy

ANDY: If you care for someone, it's normal to feel jealous.

MARK: So if someone eyes up your girlfriend, you get upset.

ANDY: I guess anyone would, it's not like we are immune to feelings.

MARK: Does the thought of losing her disturb you?

ANDY: What a crazy question. It's obvious that if you care for a girl, you don't want to lose her.

MARK: Yes, but what happens if she gets fed up and wants a change of scene, or meets someone new?

ANDY: I'd get upset; I'd try to make her stay.

MARK: So you'd sort of get her to do something against her will.

ANDY: Sure, we've known each other for years, I can't even think about her going with someone else.

MARK: So for you caring is a sort of possessing someone.

ANDY: Well, if you put it like that then love equals possession.

MARK: We've known each other for years and for a while now you've slackened off visiting your mother haven't you?

ANDY: What's my mother got to do with it? She used to breathe down my neck all the time, checking on me constantly. I could put up with it as a kid but not as an adult; I have the right to live my life.

MARK: Yeah, I agree with that. Do you think your mother cares for you?

ANDY: Sure, in her own way.

MARK: But she's kind of possessive?

ANDY: Yes, possessive and over-protective.

MARK: So, your mum cares for you but she's possessive and that irritates you, right?

ANDY: Yes, she irritates me.

MARK: So maybe your mum thinks like you, she thinks that love equals possession. Therefore for you it's ok to possess, but not to be possessed.

In the pattern we see the phases of 'possession':

1) We like someone, we feel fine when we are together.
2) We wish to see the more often.
3) When we don't get together we get upset.
4) We develop fear of losing that person.
5) We become possessive.
6) We make the assumption that love means possession.

If we do not accept this position then the affirmation: *WE DO NOT HAVE THE RIGHT TO POSSESS ANYONE* is true.

ANDY: They are two entirely different situations, loving a woman is not the same as loving your son or daughter.

MARK: Ok, they might be different. You said you mother wants to see more of you; now that she's a widow.

ANDY: Yeah, she says she needs me and when I go round she

drowns me with her anxiety and gives me stuff to do.

MARK: Maybe your father used to handle her anxiety and resolve her daily stuff?

ANDY: Yes, she always leaned a lot on dad, now she leans on me.

MARK: So your mum counts on you now?

ANDY: She counts exclusively on me.

MARK: Sorry if I go back to what I was saying about you and your girlfriend. I'm just trying to get things clear. When you have issues you talk to her, and you count on her to handle the daily stuff right?

ANDY: Yes, but I do the same for her.

MARK: Ok, but anyway she satisfies some of your needs and, if she weren't there anymore who would do that?

ANDY: For sure I'd be upset, I'd probably react.

MARK: So, someone is indispensable because they fill up the empty spaces and therefore the less self-sufficient we are the more we need someone. I remember a friend of mine who got really depressed when his wife died. He stopped eating and really went to pieces. People would say 'He must have really loved his wife' and 'See how they live for each over'. Actually, his wife filled up his void, he depended on her so much that when she died he couldn't handle his own life.

Possession could depend on our own shortcomings. Let's see:

1. A person fills our void (for example, inability to live alone).
2. That person becomes essential to us; it has become routine.
3. Difficulty arises in modifying the routine when there is no alternative behaviour to execute.
4. We miss that person, depression sets in.
5. We are unable to pull out if it because it was the 'other' satisfying our needs.

If we expect others to satisfy our needs, if we need constant praise and approval, we will never be able to choose. Choice that arises from a need is not a choice, it is an obligation. It is fundamental *TO COUNT ONLY ON YOURSELF.*

In the chapter on expectations we saw how Josh was thoroughly ill at ease on his own and only the presence of a companion would attenuate his discomfort. Being unable to choose between being alone or starting a relationship he was forced to choose the latter. He successively feared losing the person and thus became possessive.

Possessiveness and pride

In Andy and Mark's conversation we hear Andy say: 'We've known each other for years so I can't imagine she'd leave me for someone else'. Andy now lives alone and although he still sees Clara, he has his own life and interests.

MARK: I know you live an independent life and don't feel you have to justify your actions to your girlfriend.
ANDY: It's true; I've depended on my mother for so long, I don't want to depend on anyone now.
MARK: I get how you need your independence, but do you accept your girlfriend's independence.
ANDY: What do you mean 'her independence'?
MARK: Well, now you want your friends and your interests and you don't want anyone breathing down your neck. Yet you check her out, for example you ask her where she's going or who she's seen.
ANDY: Sure, I check her out, but I'm discreet, she likes it like that.

MARK: Did you ask her if she likes it?

ANDY: I just know she does, if it bothered her, she'd tell me.

MARK: And if she were to say that it *did* bother her, what would you do?

ANDY: I guess I'd think she had something to hide.

MARK: So you don't trust her?

ANDY: Well, only up to a point.

MARK: I don't get you, or you trust her or you don't.

ANDY: You make it all sound so easy; the reality is not so black and white.

MARK: You know that I'm easy going, as long as everyone is happy. Does having even the slightest doubt make you feel good?

ANDY: It would be worse if I didn't know; when I do, I'm fine.

MARK: So you have to control things to be happy?

ANDY: Now I really don't understand you. If you like someone, it's normal to be a bit jealous.

MARK: But what does being jealous do for you? If you are, do you feel better?

ANDY: It's not that I feel better being jealous, but it's normal, I can't do anything different.

MARK: Therefore jealousy is the same as mistrust, right?

ANDY: It could be.

MARK: We were talking about trust. Does trust mean that you can judge and decide if someone else's behaviour is correct or not, that is, if that person does what pleases you? I mean do we behave as we are expected to or do we wait for them to accept our behaviour?

ANDY: Well if you put it like that then trust doesn't exist.

MARK: I think it is difficult to understand ourselves, our weaknesses and predict our behaviour. We start from self-acceptance and accepting that others do as they believe correct.

Then, if that behaviour is not in line with our expectations, we shouldn't get angry; we can talk about it, and find a compromise. If we can't find a compromise then find a way to go our own separate ways without the stress. Trust can be the security that someone gives us. But if we trust in ourselves we don't need it from the other. If our pride creates upset when the other doesn't behave as we expect, and in doing so, touches upon those values they believe in, for example trust, it means they depend on someone else for their wellbeing.

This conversation touched on trust, jealousy and pride. These three terms channel into possessiveness. When we lose the trust we placed in someone, we are uncomfortable; if a partner starts giving more attention to others, we are jealous and we get upset. If we have a high opinion of ourselves, that is, we are *too* proud, and find our partner is looking at someone else, we feel our self- image undermined and we feel bad. Therefore *POSSESSIVENESS EQUALS UPSET.*

Being possessed

We saw how Andy is possessive of his girlfriend, but does not accept that she is the same with him; if the situation is fine for both, no problem. Often, though, if our partner is not possessive, we infer that they don't care for us. This happens when we start from the assumption that love equals possession.

Mark has been going out with Anna for about six months. Mark is happy with how it is going and is not possessive or jealous. Anna, on the other hand, has always struggled to accept Mark's way of being.

ANNA: You remember I used to go out with Geoff, before I met you? I caught up with him yesterday' (Anna is observing Mark to see if he shows any signs of jealousy, therefore that he cares for her).

MARK: Ah! Was it nice to see him? I suppose it must have been; you told me you had a great relationship.

ANNA: Yes it was good; he told me he still looks out for me.

MARK: That great! It's nice to know someone still cares for you.

ANNA: Does it bother you knowing that?

MARK: Absolutely not! I'm happy for you! Why should it bother me if I know it was something nice for you?

ANNA: I don't get you, how would you feel if I said I was going back to him, would it bother you?

MARK: If you want to go back to Geoff, it would be because you think you will be happier with him, so it's your problem, not mine. It's you who has to make the choice. I'm really happy with you, but I wouldn't go against your decision. It's not up to me to decide.

ANNA: I you told me you were going to leave me for another girl, I'd do everything to keep you.

MARK: And what would you gain? You'd only get upset.

ANNA: But at least I'd have tried.

MARK: I see it differently. If you care for someone, you like to know that they are happy, whatever they do. I don't see why I should get angry.

I know my reasoning is hard to accept, but it keeps us from getting upset. Events shouldn't control us; we have to control the events. When you are upset, it's because someone else has control. Therefore BE HAPPY FOR OTHERS' HAPPINESS.

Possessiveness and the past

Andy and Mark are back in conversation; Andy wants to change, he's been stung too many times expecting things others were unable to give him.

ANDY: You know what? It upsets me when Clara talks about her past relationships. I know it's irrational, but it gets to me, so I've asked her not to tell me anything.

MARK: Does it bother you to know that you weren't the only guy in her life? Is that what you mean?

ANDY: Yes, exactly, I know it's absurd.

MARK: It's as if Clara's past doesn't exist, but you know you can't do anything about that. The more we refuse a thought, the more it haunts us; to stop thinking about something we have to accept it. We can try to find out what it is that stops us from accepting a given thought.

ANDY: Maybe I'm being presumptuous.

MARK: What do you mean by presumptuous?

ANDY: I guess I think too highly of myself, maybe I want total control over Clara, over her past, present and future. Now that I think about it, if I'm not able to predict my own behaviour, how can I be sure about what others are doing, and moreover, how can I presume they will live up to my expectations.

MARK: So you are telling me that you'd like to try and accept the thought that Clara has had a past?

ANDY: I guess rationally it's the only thing to do, to face up to a relationship, even if it's not easy.

Let's analyse a scheme which highlights the characteristics of an inacceptable thought.

It is inacceptable to think that someone could have a life independent from us:

1) The thought is unsettling.
2) How do we reduce discomfort?
3) Control that person, source of our discomfort.
4) Executing control momentarily reduces discomfort.
5) A new inacceptable thought increases discomfort.
6) We need to control the situation again.

Starting from an unacceptable thought we develop a circular behaviour between the thought and the person's control.

Possessiveness and free time

Mark and Anna are still together. As in every relationship there have their ups and downs:

ANNA: You go skiing every weekend. You know I don't like skiing, if you stayed in the city we could do things together, I'm always left on my own.

MARK: I'm sorry you get so bored here at home; can't you find something to do that you enjoy?

ANNA: You know, seeing as we've been seeing each other for several months now, I'd like to be able to do things with you at the weekend; we hardly ever can during the week! A relationship is great when we do things together.

MARK: When I met you I told you all about my interests, I told you skiing was something I love, I've done it since I was a kid, but I understand you don't enjoy it.

ANNA: But you use every free moment for your own hobbies.

MARK: True, so would it be ok for you if we spent one weekend
a month together?

ANNA: It would be better than nothing.

MARK: I don't mind doing that. But I believe it would be better
for you to find something you like doing, because if I am
your only interest, I feel loaded with a responsibility I can't
handle.

ANNA: But don't you like hanging out with me?

MARK: I love being with you, but I also enjoy being with my
friends. If I hung out only with you it would mean I've got
no other interests, which wouldn't be true.

At this point Anna must accept (or not) Mark's statement.
She shouldn't be envious of Mark's independence, interests
and friends. In the couple, some things you do together and
others you don't. Doing so prevents the rapport from breaking
down.

Misappropriation

A writer gets a colleague to read some short stories he has written.

After a few weeks the colleague returns the work explaining
'They are a delightful and interesting read, only a bit difficult
to understand. Why don't you get someone else's opinion?'

After a few months we find the stories have been published.
The colleague has sent them to the editors in his name.

A friend of the writer whose work had been 'stolen' asked
him if he had filed charges.

'Why should I?' was the author's reply, 'I created and wrote
them, this guy has only got them published'.

I caught sight of my friend who owns a taxi service. He is coming out of a bar with another man in lively conversation. I think I've seen the man before: it must be one of his ex-employees who used to steal petrol from the taxis at night. When I catch up with my friend I ask him if the man I saw him with was really his ex-employee. 'Yes' he replied. 'So how come you were happily chatting to him after he'd been stealing your petrol' I ask. The simply reply was 'He's a nice guy'.

It may appear in these two cases exemplify a passive behaviour. However, it is not always necessary to be in competition, sometimes we can choose not to compete.

For example we can be criticized and insulted in public and still keep our cool, that is, we don't accept provocation.

So when can we emit that?

When we know that we *can* compete, in so much as we have already behaved in the same way in similar situations.

Selfishness

Let's try to define selfishness. Many people believe selfishness means doing exactly your own thing without considering anyone else. We hear phrases like 'He only thinks about himself' or 'If I ask him to do something for me he always refuses, he's so selfish' or 'I end up doing everything'. This is not really a definition of selfishness, it is somewhat ambiguous.

So what does the statement 'Doing exactly your own thing without considering anyone else', really mean? Take the first part 'doing your own thing': for sure it can't be that doing your own thing could harm others.

But providing we are not harming anyone, the statement 'Doing your own thing', loses its negative connotation. What do we mean by 'Selfish people do not consider anyone else'? I ask if minding your own business or suffering for someone else's pain really helps. We realize that the ingrained concern in emotional responses is not of help in resolving a situation or friend.

Therefore we cannot accept the statement: 'Selfish people do not consider others.

Often others are blamed of selfishness when issuing that which, from the outside, is considered unacceptable behaviour. By doing so we expect others to behave *we* please. However if we commit violence for our own end we are indeed selfish. So who blames for selfishness, is himself selfish. Selfishness is therefore: *the desire to change someone else to their own advantage.*

Selfishness and significant other

Let's look at a couple, married for fourteen years with a son of thirteen. The husband, forty, is very busy at work, his business is in constant development, he also is actively interested in politics. His wife, thirty-five, is a housewife. They are at lunch when her husband starts talking.

HUSBAND: I've invited two of my employees with their wives to dinner. We'll be taking shop.

WIFE: You could have told me earlier, I've got a parents' meeting at school, and I want to be there because our son is having issues with come subjects. I don't know if I'll have time to prepare dinner.

HUSBAND: I certainly won't have time to prepare myself. How come you can't get your act together to do the things you should, instead of telling me, as always, you have a lot to do? It's just a matter of organization.

WIFE: How come you always underestimate my job? (After his wife's assault the husband starts giving emotional responses, she does not feel understood so tries to justify herself.)

HUSBAND: You've never got used to real work, it's your parents fault, and you've been spoilt. You don't know what real work is. (The husband feels right in making these accusations.)

Let's see the husband's thought processes:

1) I work hard for my family.
2) I guarantee the family's economic wellbeing.
3) I am right in expecting something back; I shouldn't always have to think of everything.
4) My wife is selfish; she's not there when I need her.

WIFE: Okay, I'll get dinner together. At most I'll skip the school meeting.

His wife agrees, but is submissive; she tries blaming the husband with the phrase 'At most I'll skip the school meeting.' This phrase can have a dual effect. In the first case the husband, feeling guilty, will reply, 'Okay I'll try to move the dinner to another day and let you know in good time'. This response in this case, is unlikely; more predictably, we will hear the aggressive response: 'Then don't go to school!'

Let's see how the wife could have dealt with this scenario, and consider three possible answers. In the first response, the wife makes no compromise:

HUSBAND: I've invited...
WIFE: I'm sorry you've told me so late, I already have an appointment at the school this afternoon, and I won't make it in time to prepare dinner.

This type of response given to an aggressive person is likely to increase their aggressiveness. So the wife must be able to withstand an 'attack' from the husband, who could start blaming. For example:

HUSBAND: I hardly ever ask you anything, now that I need

you, you're not helping. You only think about yourself.

WIFE: I'm sorry to have created this. But please let me know when we have guests to dinner two or three days before. I hate having to do everything in a hurry.

Most likely the husband will get even more irritated. In this case, the wife must not give in and must maintain her position. We will see any other eventual price the wife will pay using a similar response.

Second reply:

HUSBAND: I've invited…

WIFE: I realize the commitment this evening with your employees is important to you. For my part, I have to go to a school reunion this afternoon. I'll also try to fit the dinner in. In future let me know a few days beforehand, because it bothers me to do everything in a hurry.

Here the wife is making a compromise.

Third answer:

HUSBAND: I've invited...

WIFE: I realize the commitment this evening with your employees is important to you. For my part, I want go to the school meeting and I don't know how long they'll keep me there. But we could easily solve the problem by ordering some food from the Deli, maybe starters and sweet, and I can prepare some pasta. It'll cost a bit more, but less than going out to eat, and the food will be good.

The wife makes a compromise, but the husband has to pay the price.

Which of the three answers seems more appropriate?
a) With the first the wife does not accept a compromise. We predict an increase of aggressiveness from her husband. This aggressive behaviour will persist in time and increase in intensity.

Observe the following steps:

1) The wife begins 'competing' with her husband. She is not going to passively succumb.
2) The husband is surprised by his wife's change of behaviour. He didn't expect it. They have been married for fourteen years, and his wife has always been submissive.
3) The husband does not accept a competitive wife, so becomes more aggressive, blames her and puts her down, hoping thereby to obtain submissive behaviour.
4) The wife continues to assert her right.
5) The husband further increases his aggressiveness.
6) Stalemate. The wife wants to establish herself in her own right as a person, so her husband is obliged to change. The husband doesn't want to change their relationship.

What could the eventual result be?

Probably you will find yourself in a state of perpetual stress. The wife wants to assert her rights, while the husband doesn't want to lose his 'privileges'. The sudden change in the wife does not reflect a change in her husband. The couple are now speaking two different and incomprehensible languages. Once discomfort increases to a certain level within a couple and there is no foreseeable solution, the couple often separate. In this case the wife is not working from her husband's 'operating level'; she has jumped some of the steps. It's like teaching algebra to a child without checking they know the basics of maths.

b) With the second response in which the wife make a compromise, but shows her discomfort we see two phases:

1) The wife communicates her discomfort but behaves exactly as her husband wishes.
2) The husband pays a limited personal price, That is, knowledge that his wife feels uncomfortable.

Now in this situation the husband is not motivated to change. His wife, as similar situations appear, remains calm, explains her needs without expecting her husband to change. She is happy with a tiny result. She is starting from her husband's operating level and persistence gets positive results, although often doing so she could pay a high price. It is tiresome having to constantly repeat oneself.

c) The third answer, although similar to the second, tends to create a higher price for the husband. The wife always starts from the husband's level, but in this case, creates two prices to pay: the first, by communicating her own psychological discomfort, and the second, of economic type. This third answer if 'played' carefully, that is, without having the husband pay too high a price, can accelerate the modification process.

Worrying about others

ANDY: Unselfish people care for others. I don't think you really care much about anyone.
MARK: You mean that selfless people are glad to help others?

ANDY: Yes, I mean that.

MARK: So a selfless person has some benefit in helping others.

ANDY: That doesn't seem right to me, selfless people do things *only* for others.

MARK: But if you see someone is sick or needs help you would worry, wouldn't you?

ANDY: Of course I would, I hate to see people suffer.

MARK: So if you helped someone in trouble then you'd feel fine.

ANDY: Yes, I'd be pleased with what I had done.

MARK: I'm trying to get this clear. Seeing others suffering upsets you, and you would try to ease their discomfort, which would make *you* happy and put an end to your discomfort.

ANDY: In any case, I'm helping someone.

MARK: I agree. But it also seems to me that if you don't help even one person you get upset anyway, right? So that's your way of behaving; helping others relieves your discomfort, so you're forced to helping people just to keep happy.

ANDY: Your reasoning is cynical. You make everything sound so simple.

MARK: I don't see the problem. If you're happy with that, fine by me. I'm glad to know that you're happy with yourself.

ANDY: I'm trying to explain that what you're doing isn't right; it sounds like you think only for yourself.

MARK: That is, you mean to say that I don't care for others?

ANDY: Yes, exactly!

MARK: Don't worry about me, I'm fine. It's not a problem for me, maybe the problem is yours: *you* are worried about my behaviour and would like *me* to change. Why should I change, if it's all fine for me?

In this dialogue Andy is assuming that an unselfish person

cares for others. Mark supports the idea that selflessness is not helping others to avoid experiencing discomfort. We see the following pattern:

Pattern I
1) Someone is upset.
2) We feel uncomfortable.
3) We offer to help the person:
    a. The person helped feels better, we feel better;
    b. The person does not feel better and we decide that we do the best we can to help and we feel better.

Pattern II
1) Someone is upset.
2) We do not feel uncomfortable.
3) It's a pleasure to help.
4) We do not expect anything in exchange.

The second pattern shows selflessness that does not arise from discomfort, but from pleasure. If we accept this position, then *WE MUST NOT MAKE OTHERS' PROBLEMS OUR OWN*. In any situation we have to discriminate between our and the other's problem. And if we can, or if we are happy to help others in their issues we must always remember that the problem is theirs.

Envy

Sometimes a smidgen of rancour surfaces when we see someone having success. Perhaps we would like to be in their place, achieving what they have. We believe to have the same or even greater abilities, and consider them to be lucky; we are convinced that they are unscrupulous and we are not. We find many examples to justify their success and our failure.

Envy and Work

Mark is at dinner with Geoff, a friend he hasn't seen for eight years. They were at University together; Geoff later moved to work in another city.

MARK: You were saying that the job didn't go well.
GEOFF: No, not at all, but that's often happens in large companies.
MARK: Didn't you like it?

GEOFF: I liked the work, but not the environment.

MARK: How do you mean didn't you like the environment?

GEOFF: You wouldn't understand because you've never worked in a large industry.

MARK: Tell me anyway, I'm interested.

GEOFF: I gave it my all, but I saw some people rapidly making a career with much less effort.

MARK: So you saw people riding over you who, in your opinion, were not worth as much.

GEOFF: Yes, exactly, and it hurts to see them moving forward having absolutely no personal worth.

MARK: You had hoped to make a career, hadn't you?

GEOFF: Of course I had, at least to see some reward for my efforts.

MARK: Have you always worked for the same the same employer?

GEOFF: No, I changed, three years in the first company, and five in the second.

MARK: Was it equally bad in both?

GEOFF: Yes, and the same thing repeating itself; less deserving people just riding over the top of me.

MARK: And that gets to you, right?

GEOFF: Obviously! You work to get recognition. Like I said, you wouldn't understand because you've never experienced industry.

MARK: In these eight years, how many people have gone forward with their career?

GEOFF: Two in the first place and three in the second. We all started at the same level then the others got ahead, while I was left behind.

MARK: Among those five that got ahead, don't you think anyone had better skills than you?

GEOFF: If you mean like the ability to be a hypocrite, then
    they definitely had more skills than me. I always did my job
    honestly, but, if I saw something that I didn't like, I always
    spoke out and I've paid the price for being honest.
MARK: So you're can't find a way to emerge, and this makes
    you uncomfortable, right?
GEOFF: Yes, it's the industrial structure that doesn't allow for it.
MARK: Perhaps better to say that it didn't allow *you* to emerge.
GEOFF: No, people who work seriously don't emerge.

Geoff failed to achieve the goals he set for himself. This is
a source of discomfort; he is in a vicious circle, even changing
jobs left him with the same problem. Geoff has made some mistakes:

1. Cognitive: he considers himself a 'good' worker, it is the
    others who don't appreciate his work.
2. Emotional: not having achieved the goals he set for himself
    creates his 'anger'.
3. Behavioural: he tends to criticize others' work.

Geoff's behaviour creates the hostile environment. The less
he is able to manage the work environment the more he becomes
aggressive with those colleagues climbing the career ladder.
 We could imagine that Geoff will not change: he is too centred
on others' behaviour to see what is wrong in his own behaviour.
What are the benefits that derive from envy? Actually, none
whatsoever! Remember *THE RESENTFUL DO NOT CHANGE.*
When we feel anger, we are no longer able to discriminate; we
cannot identify others' positive behaviour and only see the negative aspects.

Envy And Friends

Marina and Claudia started high school together. Marina is extrovert; she has good social skills and is comfortable in most situations. She is always invited to all social events and has a stream of admirers. Claudia is a pretty girl, but finds communication difficult and therefore tends to subtract herself from social situations; her friend interprets her behaviour as refusal and thus calls and invites are ever less frequent. At the start Marina and Claudia hung out a lot, studied together and shared their secrets. It was always Marina to initiate conversation and open up to her friend, while Claudia would sit back and listen. As the years go by, Claudia is even more withdrawn, dedicating her time to study and ending up among the top scholars. School gratifies her, but only in part; she sees her friend doing well at school but also with many interests and friends.

The two start seeing each less of each other. Marina finds it difficult now to confide in Claudia, and when she tries, Claudia clams up. Their conversation takes on a formal tone: they talk about school. Claudia bears a grudge against Marina and tells me: 'She hung out with me because it was convenient, now she has loads of friends we hardly ever see each other, I might as well put an end to this false friendship.'

Take a look at the conversation between Marina and Claudia:

MARINA: So the maths exam went well this morning?

CLAUDIA: Yes, I studied really hard. (Claudia lets the subject drop).

MARINA: I'm sure you did, you always do.

CLAUDIA: You know how it is, when you have nothing else to do (Starts blaming, insinuating her friend is neglecting her).

MARINA: Hey! But I'm always inviting you here and there; you
    never want to come.
CLAUDIA: What's the point? As soon as we get to the venue,
    you disappear off with your other friends, and I end up alone
    (Claudia continues to blame).
MARINA: See, I go to parties because I enjoy meeting new peo-
    ple and finding friends.
CLAUDIA: It's easy for you. When you get there everybody
    swarms around you, it's always up to me to go and dig people
    out, *and that* really bothers me.
MARINA: I don't see the problem, if you like to meet people,
    just wander up and say hello!

Marina and Claudia have frequent conversations of this
type and, at the end of this one; Claudia ends up ever more
convinced that Marina is not a friend. However, Claudia is
left feeling ill-at-ease and disturbed by Marina's social success.
Every time she tries making Marina feel guilty, in the hope that
her friend's behaviour will change. Claudia does not look at
her own incompetence; even though it is exactly that making
her feel awkward. She is too focused on her friend's social
achievements. So *LOOK AFTER YOURSELF AND DON'T WOR-
RY ABOUT OTHERS' SUCCESS.*

Envy and cars

Mark and Geoff are out walking and spot a flash car go past.

GEOFF: Did you see that car? It's that storekeeper's. The guy
    has opened a whole chain and made it rich in no time. He's
    a total moron.

MARK: Does it bother you that he got rich?

GEOFF: It seems to me that it's the wise-guys who get rich. They don't take any other values into account.

MARK: What other values?

GEOFF: Education, intelligence. Like the only worthwhile this is being rich.

MARK: And that bothers you, doesn't it?

GEOFF: It bothers me a lot, and I don't understand why you don't even flinch; your job certainly hasn't made you rich or famous.

MARK: Getting rich or famous is not my problem and I do a job that I like and I'm happy with. Maybe I'll want something different in the future or find new interests and some new input, but right now I'm not even thinking about it. So what do *you* obtain by getting irritated about the shopkeeper? Nothing, I think.

GEOFF: No, It doesn't get me anything, it just bothers me.

MARK: Probably the shopkeeper started out, set himself some goals, like wanting to grow his business, and therefore, earn more. There are many people out there who may have wanted the same thing, but haven't succeeded; you have to admit he's done well. What are your goals?' Although for me, you don't necessarily have to reach some goal at any price, you can be just fine with what you've got and be happy about it.

GEOFF: I told you my goals: I want to emerge and move up in my career, but external events haven't allowed me to do so. I studied for years, for what? Then, you happen to see that a shopkeeper makes it rich in only a few years... I just don't understand how the world works! And I don't understand how you can be content with what you've got, if that were so, there would be no place for progress.

MARK: See Geoff, a few years ago my uncle Antonio died. As a kid I used to love going to see him, we would spend whole afternoons playing chess. It was so good being with him; he was just so happy with his life. He was a printer and good at his job. One day a very influential friend of his, asked him to move to another city to work for a certain industry, where his skills would be greatly appreciated; he would also have earned much more. Uncle Antonio had replied, 'I love my city, I love fishing in the rivers nearby and mushrooming in the woods, all this is enough for me.

Resentment

Resentment underlies aggressive behaviour that does not manifest through direct attack, it is unexpressed anger. In any case, those who bear a grudge feel discomfort, and emotion which can persist in time.

Therefore, the question is why do we bear grudges if it makes us feel uncomfortable?

It is hard not to feel resentment, but it *is easy* to arouse such feelings when we suffer others, when we mistakenly place trust in someone or when we want a person to change.

The silent husband

The husband becomes taciturn and surly when his wife doesn't behave as he expects. His silence lasts for several days. He hopes, in doing so, his wife will change, and understand her error. They had been married for twelve years.

We see the situation that triggers her husband's silence.

WIFE: I would like to move that sideboard today, so help me; I am really convinced it will look great under the window.
HUSBAND: But I like where it is now and I don't see why we should move it.
WIFE: Well, let's just give it a try, and then decide if it's okay.
HUSBAND: You always get your own way!

The husband begins to help his wife, but is angry with her, because he feel imposed upon. He does the job uninterestedly. His nonverbal behaviour decries a flat refusal. He moves abruptly, grumbling and complaining. The wife doesn't comment or shows impatience, because her husband often behaves this way.

WIFE: What do you think now about the sideboard under the window? It looks much better there to me.
HUSBAND: If you like it, fine.

As he speaks, the husband slopes off, without even considering the sideboard's new position. After which, he doesn't utter a single word for the rest of the day.

Her husband's resentment manifests itself in an accusatory silence. All the while he is angry with her, meanwhile enduring his discomfort. His wife continues as normal. Her husband is at fault:

1) He believes his wife should accept his statement: 'I like it where it is now'.
2) He believes to have suffered his wife's 'violence'.
3) He does not accept his wife point of view thus is not open to change his opinion.

The husband feels his wife should be 'punished' for the way she behaves. The husband is resentful towards his wife and becomes silent, hoping thereby to make her feel guilty and therefore, modify her behaviour. It seems absurd that we can be angry for such an irrelevant situation. But indeed, often a simple situation that we believe we have 'suffered' can trigger resentfulness.

Although by nature the husband, having a tendency to blame, does possess a certain sense of humour and comes to me saying: 'Sometimes, after starting in my silences, I actually forget what my grudge was about, but I don't talk to her anyway, because I reckon that if I wasn't taking to her, there must have been a good reason.' Dryly admitting his behaviour, which claims to have learned from his mother, he explained that in his youth, when he did something which his mother believed to be incorrect, he had to endure her long silences.

Resentment and friends

We have started a job as requested. After about six months, we realize we need a co-worker to deal with a part of it. We ask a friend we know to be competent and who has adequate experience. The friend is presented to whoever has commissioned the job and the collaboration begins. He proves to be skilled and solves a whole series of operational problems. After a further six months, the collaboration has proved fruitful for all concerned. Who appointed the job is very satisfied and with this, the friend feels free to directly contact the appointee for continuation of the work. We find out about their agreement after the contract is signed. We, of course, were excluded from the new agreement. Now we see two possible responses to this situation.

The first could be anger and resentment towards the friend. The second, no resentment, and in addition, we can consider the situation as a useful learning opportunity. This latter will surely appear difficult to execute, in particular when a friend has 'betrayed' you. Let's first ask whether the first response can be of any use to us: The fact if that the only result we obtain by showing resentfulness and anger is that we feel huge emotional discomfort, and when it gets really uncomfortable, it is difficult to make valid decisions. We see a sequence of thoughts that brings us, in this case, to feel resentment:

1) I was the one to give him the job and I knew the appointee.
2) The friend made direct contact with the appointee without consulting me.
3) I would never have done anything similar, friends don't do that.
4) I would have never expected him to do such a thing.
5) I don't want to have anything to do with this person in the future.

Now take a look at the new sequence:

1) The friend is skilled at his job.
2) What bothers me is that he didn't ask me before making the agreement.

We need to ask some questions:
— How can I avoid this happening again?
— Could I need this person or someone like him in the future?

If we need co-workers for our business, it is essential that this situation does not occur again, so what should we do? Simply, we must establish a written agreement with our eventual collaborator, making clear that co-workers cannot make arrangements directly with who commissions the work. Thus we cannot feel anger or resentment, and we will continue to consider our friend skilful and competent, *we* were wrong for not establishing clear grounds at the outset. We avoid saying:

— I would never have done a similar thing.
— I did not expect this from a friend.

As we have seen in other cases, the error is in focusing attention on others, making them the cause of our distress.

The goodbye

ANDY: You remember Josh, the guy I met a couple of years ago? Did you know he had really bad-mouthed me, telling all in sundry that I am untrustworthy!

MARK: I'm sorry to hear that. Did you clear things up?

ANDY: What is there to clear up? His behaviour is unacceptable. So that's the end of our friendship. If he happens to cross my path, I'm not even going to say hello.

MARK: So now you're really angry with him.

ANDY: Of course I am, after what he did.

MARK: Yes, but are telling me something somebody else told you.

ANDY: Yes, it's sufficient isn't it?

MARK: So when you think about it you are bitter and really pissed off, right?

ANDY: You bet! I'd like to what you would have done in my place.

MARK: Actually, something similar happened to me; I was accused of badmouthing a guy I used go running with called Sandro. Later another friend asked me if we still see each other and I explained, (seeing as I don't go running anymore) we didn't have the common interest anymore, so I rarely saw him. A few days later I caught up with Sandro and I found out our mutual friend had told him I didn't hang out with him anymore because he was a bore! I was really taken aback, then, on second thoughts, I realized that my sentence about not having a common interest, had been loosely interpreted'

ANDY: But here your friend had misunderstood; my case is different.

MARK: Yes but perhaps if Sandro hadn't wanted me to clear things up, I'd have been none the wiser.

ANDY: But if you had actually told your friend that you didn't see Sandro anymore because he's a bore, what would have happened?

MARK: Sandro would have spoken to me all the same, and I would have explained why I found him boring.

Resentment may depend on a fear of judgement:

1) We are criticized (in Andy's case it is indirect criticism).
2) We are quickly upset when we hear about the criticism.
3) We are angered by the person slating us.
4) We feel bear a grudge and avoid future contact.

We must learn to accept different points of view and work out if the information can be of use; we can only judge our own behaviour.

Interpretation

Critical situations often make objectiveness an issue: we tend to interpret.

A husband and wife are my clients and their relationship is very 'tense.' They both describe the same situation at separate meetings.

She explains: 'Last night I went to bed before my husband, he carried on watching TV. I was half asleep when he came to bed. He gets in near to me and, as I moved, I accidentally kicked him. So he got up, irritated, and went back to watching TV, leaving me wide awake'. The husband's version goes like this: 'Last night my wife went to bed before me, and I came up soon after. I realize she is not asleep so I cuddle up to her, but she deliberately kicks me. I guessed she doesn't want me near so I got up again and went to watch the TV. Next day, neither mentioned the episode, and as we speak, there is clearly a mutual resentment between the two. Each spouse gives their own version of the event; the wife is angry with her husband for his lack of 'sensitivity'; her husband believes that his wife wants to deliberately snub him. We are wasting our time if we want to understand which of them is right. There is tension between the couple, communication is impossible. By not communicating, the tendency is to 'interpret' the other's behaviour; *any* other behaviour emitted is decoded as a 'deliberate' attack. In these situations we identify:

1) Selective focusing on other's negative behaviour.
2) Interpretation of behaviour and activation of thoughts like, 'He/she does it just to upset me'.
3) Resentment towards the other.

4) Absence of dialogue and therefore of possible explanations.

5) Increase of selective focus on the other's negative aspects.

6) Validation of own hypothesis, namely: 'He/she does just to upset me'.

So we have created a vicious circle: Interpretation- resentment-interpretation; all which prevents clarification. Based on the above situation, the couple have identified the 'errors' that did not allow them to interact properly and thus have learned:

1) To immediately sort out any issues.

2) To focus on other's positive aspects and avoid manipulative criticism.

Suspicion

A married lady receives a call, a voice tells her: 'I know that your husband has a lover, you'd better check it out'. The lady asks who is speaking and the voice replies 'a friend'. How do we behave? We can act towards our partner in different ways:

1) Say nothing.

2) Say nothing, but check them out.

3) Say nothing, get someone else to check them out.

4) Talk to partner to try and find out if they have something to hide.

5) Talk to friends for advice.

6) Talk with them, just to mention the phone call.

7) Talk with them so they can give me advice on how to respond if they call again.

8) Talk with them, because I want them to say it's not true.

How would you behave?

Personally I'd choose number 6. I'd also consider number 7. But choosing requires:

— Not thinking about the call.
— Not asking any questions.
— Accepting the response.

You can also choose number 1, providing you completely ignore the phone call. If you do have doubts, you are forced to choose other solutions. Doubt is always accompanied by distress, which in this case, can be induced by possession or pride.

Sacrifice and pleasure

Giving up our plans to please someone else or carrying on the family business because your parents want you to and giving up a hobby to please our partner. These are some examples of sacrifice. Sacrifice is focused on others; you give up something that is important in favour of someone else. Sacrifice may arise from 'having to be' a good wife, a good son or a good friend. To be a 'good wife' means putting the children and husband's needs before our own. But if duty or sacrifice creates discomfort, why do we insist in doing it? Can sacrifice be a pleasure? If sacrifice *can* be pleasure, it shouldn't make us uncomfortable.

Duty to give

ANDY: It's really hard to have true friends. After a while you realize that friendship is often one-sided.
MARK: What do you mean by one-sided?
ANDY: I'm sure you've been in a situation where you've given so much for so little in return.

MARK: Yes, it can happen, but what happened in your case?

ANDY: I've been working for several months with a colleague who I considered a friend. When I saw he was having issues at work I always tried to help him; I used to stay late at work to give him a hand to get stuff finished. Then two days ago I asked him to help me finish a job and he tells me he has no time and goes away.

MARK: It was your colleague who asked you to stop to help?

ANDY: Well, sometimes I offered myself, other times he asked me.

MARK: Did you always stop to help even when you didn't want to or if you had something more important to do?

ANDY: I stopped more than once to help him, though I didn't really want to. I wasn't even feeling well once, but I stayed behind for another two hours.

MARK: But if you didn't want to help, who forced you to do it?

ANDY: No-one, it seems normal to want to help a friend in need.

MARK: So you're saying that you consider your colleague a friend and therefore your duty to help him, is that it?

ANDY: Yes, in friendship that's what you do.

MARK: I think differently. Earlier you asked me if I had ever 'given' a lot to a friend; it's hard to give an answer because I never quantify what I give to a friend and never think of a friendship in terms of cost-benefit. If I 'give' something to a friend it is because I wish to do so, and it gives me pleasure. It's difficult to quantify how much pleasure I have in giving. I never use the terms obligation or duty for my friends because if I did so, I would tend to expect something in return for what I give and giving without getting anything in return would make me feel bad. So if I 'gave' 100 is because I wanted to, and if the friend has 'given me' 10, I have gained 110.

Otherwise in your terms I'd still be owed 90, right?

Andy's behaviour is not unusual; however, it tends to create expectations. Let's take a look at Andy's errors:

1) Friendship implies duty.
2) Duty is 'giving' to a friend.
3) You cannot refuse anything to a friend.
4) You expect the friend to behave in the same way with us.
5) If this doesn't happen, it means they are not friends.
6) Therefore it is my right to terminate the friendship.

Therefore *DO NOT SAY: 'I GAVE YOU....(AND YOU DIDN'T GIVE ME).*

Appearances

Have you ever tried to follow a diet? It can be difficult. Have you ever gone to the gym to keep fit? It can be tedious. Dieting or exercising in the gym can be a major sacrifice. But can we turn it into pleasure?

I meet a friend I haven't seen for several months, I see he's put on weight and say. 'It looks like you could do with losing a few pounds'. He replies: 'You're right, I've put on weight. Do you remember how I was a few years ago? I need to lose about 40 pounds. I've already tried dieting, I lose a few pounds then keep putting them back on; I also tried exercising, but that just makes me hungry. Yes, I really should do something'

'But' - I say - 'you've already tried and perhaps find it too difficult to stick to any diet a normal diet.'

'Yes, that's right' – he replies – 'It's such sacrifice to

keep myself in check. I just can't find the motivation; when I was a bachelor I used to be more interested in my appearance; obviously being fat is not the best presentation opposite sex. I need to find some sort of motivation to help me keep in shape. Could you give me any advice?' 'See' - I reply – 'You say you would need motivation to keep fit, but what, exactly do you mean?'

'It could be a lady friend' - he tells me – 'or perhaps, doing work that makes me more active; it is not easy to find time to go to the gym, and dieting is difficult because I'm often away on business'. For my friend it's hard to stay in shape for the following reasons:

1) Dieting is a sacrifice.
2) Going to the gym is a sacrifice.
3) He seeks some external stimulus to induce keeping fit.
4) He tends to self-justify his lack of motivation.

It wouldn't be a problem if he were to accept things as they were, but he is dissatisfied with his appearance and he would like to be physically more efficient. His thinking pattern is:

1) Keeping fit is difficult and tiring.
2) My efforts should be compensated by rewards that come from the outside.
3) In the absence of 'external stimuli' it is useless keeping in shape.

Once again we see a vicious circle from which it is difficult to escape. In this case attention should be focused on self, not on others. If we want to improve our physical appearance we must do it *only* for ourselves. We must be able to reward ourselves through observing the results we get by progressively controlling diet and doing exercise. So the sacrifice no longer exists as it becomes a pleasure to observe the results we obtain. When you finally reach a state of physical efficiency, it becomes almost automatic to want to maintain it, and the sequence is as follows:

1) I feel perfectly fit.
2) I want to keep this 'state'.
3) If I neglect myself I am uncomfortable.
4) Discomfort diminishes if I look after myself.

Like any of life's circumstances, taking care of appearance will not bring results unless we are prepared to pay the price, and it is up to us to decide whether we want to pay it or not. In any case we do not self-justify our inaction. It depends on us to develop 'the pleasure of liking ourselves'.

Self-image

Take a look at Kevin and Martha:

Kevin is 32, confident, designer dressed, has a smart car and is definitely 'in with the in crowd'. Martha is 28, dresses down and tends not to 'appear', responding only if directly addressed. She is sweet, smiling and accommodating. What creates a bond between two such different types? Both seek to create an image of themselves through the way they dress or talk. I believe we all do this; however it can be a source of uneasiness. Kevin wants to create the image of a man who has 'made it', so he studies and copies the behaviour of people who for him have 'made it'. He is focused on the image he wants to create. Kevin divides people into two categories: those who have 'made it' and those who haven't.

I ask Kevin who the 'made it' people are. He answers, 'The ones who have achieved a high economic and social status'. Kevin tries hard to hang out with such types, he wants to learn from them and be accepted by them. The judgment of the people who 'count' is extremely important for Kevin. He does not pay the slightest attention to those he believes unimportant, indeed he criticizes them. Is it really a pleasure for Kevin to behave this way? Or does his pleasure derive exclusively from the approval he gets from others? We see the following pattern:

1) Kevin wants to 'appear'.
2) The 'made it' judgment is important to him.
3) He needs their approval.
4) He is gratified in gaining their approval.

He becomes uncomfortable without their approval, and therefore must create alternative behaviour to gain acceptance.

We see here how his pleasure derives from the approval he gets. It would be very different to saing: 'I am pleased to be among these people', from saying 'It's important for me to be with them'. There are however analogies between Kevin and Martha's behaviour. Martha too has a need to 'appear' and maintain her image as educated, respectful and accommodating. Her family has always told her that keeping a low profile is good. Martha is from a rich family and could be gratified by travel, beautiful clothes, jewellery and so on. But Martha cannot allow herself to indulge in such pleasures because doing so means for her to be 'showing off'. The family has brought her up to avoid anything that may be considered 'frivolous'. We can see how Martha's behaviour is similar to that of Kevin:

1) Martha wants to keep a low profile.
2) Her parents judgement is relevant.
3) She needs to gain their approval.
4) She obtains their approval and is gratified.

Therefore, both Kevin and Martha need to behave in a certain way to obtain external approval, and in so doing, can avoid feeling discomfort.

Need

A loved one has to leave for a few weeks and we are unhappy; we are alone at home and we want some company. We often emit certain behaviour to escape uncomfortable situations. Let's see the dialogue between Mark and his friend Andy. Mark now lives with Anna, his girlfriend. Mark has previously spoken with Andy about possession and need.

ANDY: It's been ages since I've seen you; I hear you're living with Anna now. How come you took this decision, I didn't think you wanted to get hooked up?

MARK: I'm happy with her. She's so independent, and there's mutual respect and esteem. It's like neither of us try to prevaricate.

ANDY: But you are still doing the same things, you've kept all of your hobbies and interests, even the stuff that keeps you out in the evenings?

MARK: Yes, nothing has changed, really.

ANDY: Sorry, I don't get you. For what good reason would you want to live with Anna if you just keep on doing what you've always done?

MARK: I don't see why I should change, if it's fine for me.
ANDY: But is it OK for Anna? You'll be in only once or twice a week.

MARK: Anna knows me and accepts the way I am. Obviously I accept anything that she does too.

ANDY: Does she go out without you?

MARK: A bit less than me.

ANDY: Doesn't that bother you?

MARK: A while back, Anna was preparing to go out and I felt a bit miserable. I told her it bothered me staying home alone and she said: If bothers you all we have to do is plan our evenings so when you're at home, we can be together'. I asked Anna if she was happy when I go out and she said she was actually glad to be at home on her own. I realized I was starting to need Anna, and when she wasn't around I kind of felt out of place.

ANDY: So what did you do?

MARK: I told myself that my relationship with Anna must be based on the pleasure of being with her and not on need. On nights when I know she's out, I learned to enjoy watching movies. I learned to stay home and feel good. After a while I didn't even need to watch movies.

ANDY: Wouldn't it have been easier just to ask her to stay home?

MARK: It would have been easier, but then it would have been hard to tell if I was with Anna for the pleasure of her company or because I was unable to be at home alone.

In this case Mark believes that a relationship is more valuable when it is based on mutual pleasure and not on either's needs.

Mark considers himself to be 'independent' and takes into account his way of being in his choice of partner. His preferred partner must also be 'independent,' that is, is not dependent on him.

His reasoning is as follows:

1) 'If my partner depends on me, it makes me nervous'.
2) 'I could avoid this by either trying to change my partner or trying to change myself'.

But he doesn't accept the reasoning as solution because:

1) 'If I try to change my partner it is because I want them to be different. If I try to change them, would that change be what I want it to be? Is it right to want to change a person?'
2) 'If I try to change myself it will be a great sacrifice and commitment. I would expect therefore, that my partner understands I am changing for them'.

Mark does not believe it appropriate to modify the partner, or modify himself. Therefore, Mark's partner should require and commitment on his behalf.

Changing behaviour

We have already seen how to modify nonverbal behaviour (see assertive communication). Obviously having good verbal skills is not enough to establish good interpersonal relationships or to circumvent uneasiness in the countless everyday situations we face. In any given behaviour we must always bear in mind the interaction between motor, physiological-emotional and cognitive development systems Intervention must occur on all three systems to implement modification of a consolidated behaviour.

We can develop some non-verbal and verbal skills, yet continue to experience discomfort when we feel judged. We use some verbal techniques properly, such as fogging or negative inquiry, but when we are criticized we still feel anger. If we stand in front of a mirror and observe, we can see our weight gain or if we are wearing the right tie and adjust accordingly. However, sometimes we don't see things objectively. Being able to discriminate, that is, to grasp a particular 'irregularity', may depend on our past experience and, therefore, on the selective attention that we place on a precise detail. If we decide to change our behaviour, we must carefully observe and identify the areas where we are particularly lacking and then take action.So how can we identify our shortcomings? In dealing with any situation there is always a before, during and after. If one of these three moments we feel uncomfortable, we have already identified the eventual area we may need to modify.

You may wonder if in this way we risk losing our spontaneity which could be a plausible objection to initiating any change program. I think, however, you would agree that the more behaviour skill we can master, the better we are able to manage the various situations. Moreover, if we accept the assumption that we don't have to feel discomfort, it follows that possessing more skills will correspond to a minor discomfort in the most varied situations. If a person has a reduced load of behavioural possibilities, they will have fewer choices available.

People who always give the same response in any given situation, because they have no other response available is perhaps more robotic than someone who, in the same situation, can choose from a range of resources. Conversely, the more choices of actions we have, the more we are spontaneous. Obviously, to be totally spontaneous, one would need to be free from conditioning, but, as we have seen, this is impossible.

Life's events affect us constantly, often almost passively; we see ourselves change. A dramatic event in our lives, maybe the death of a loved one, can bring rapid changes. But if we think of change as an active process, then we must be ready for change and constantly willing to learn.

Starting to change

We could also say: 'Let's *try* to change', but its better avoid using the word 'try.' If we want to learn to drive a car, we start by going to driving school, and it is assumed that by the end of lessons you will be able to drive. While at driving school we are learning to drive and at the beginning it will be difficult, but then driving becomes automatic. In this case we haven't *tried* to drive a car, we *learned* to drive. So we do things or we don't; trying is unnecessary. Saying 'I'll try' can too often be only our good intention which we never actually to achieve.

Identifying our behaviour

We have seen how social behaviour can be passive, aggressive or assertive.

As a reminder, *passive behaviour* is when we:

1) Suffer others.
2) Have difficulty in making or refusing requests.
3) Have difficulty in making or accepting compliments and communicating our feelings.
4) Need approval.
5) Depend on others' judgment.
6) Are often afraid of making mistakes.
7) Believe that others are better than us.
8) Feel uncomfortable with people who do not know well.
9) Have difficulty making decisions.
10) Feel guilty after showing aggressive behaviour.

These are just some drawbacks that may arise during inter-personal relationships. In any case, to be passive, you don't need to have all of these characteristics and consider yourself lucky if you have only three or four!

Aggressive behaviour is when we:

1) Want others to do as *we* please.
2) Never change our opinion about someone or something.
3) Decide for others without hearing their viewpoint.
4) Do not accept that we can make mistakes.
5) Never say sorry.
6) Do not listen to others as they speak.
7) Frequently interrupt during conversation.
8) Judge and criticize.
9) Use guilt-inducing or putting down strategies.
10) Consider we are the best.

If we believe to possess all these characteristics then probably a lot of people don't love us. But aggressive people don't mind not being loved; it's not their problem!

And finally, *assertive behaviour* is when we:

1) Accept other points of view.
2) Do not judge.
3) Do not put down or blame.
4) Listen to others, but decide indipendently.
5) Are ready to change opinion.
6) Do not allow for manipulation.
7) Do not believe others should do as *we* please.
8) Seek to collaborate.

9) Are able to communicate emotions or moods.
10) Appropriately self-assess.

It is really pleasant being around an assertive person: pity that there are so few of them about!

Recognizing our own behaviour style can be challenge: we can shift through all three, depending on the situation. I suggest, at least at the beginning of any behaviour modification program, to write:

1) The situation you are in.
2) Any discomfort you feel. Discomfort can be assessed on a scale of 0 to 10, where 0 indicates no discomfort and 10 maximum discomfort.
3) The kind of behaviour you issued.
4) The kind of behaviour you would have preferred to issue.

It shouldn't take too long to do this self-assessment. Soon you will be able to identify your behaviour style. Here are some examples:

1. A friend contradicts us.
2. We feel discomfort (score 3).
3a. We look at our friend down our nose, tilt our heads to one side and with a faint smile on our faces.
3b. We think: 'You're saying the usual nonsense'.
3c. We ironically reply: 'It would be better to get informed before you open your mouth'

How should we have behaved?

1. A friend contradicts us.

2. We think: 'He has a right to express an opinion'.
3. We say: 'I understand what you are saying; it's just that I see it differently'.
1. We are invited to a meeting with many people we do not know.
2. Once at the meeting, we look for the ones we do know, we find them, but they are talking to people we don't know.
3. We feel discomfort (rated 6).
4. We want to leave and say to ourselves: 'I must stop getting myself into these types of situations, next time I'll go only if I know all the guests'.
5. We seek solace alone in a corner of the room.

How could we have behaved?

1. We are invited...
2. Once at the meeting...
3. We join a group, although we feel uncomfortable.
4. We listen to what others are saying and study their facial expression.
5. As our discomfort decreases we take part in conversation.

The first example shows aggression, proof is our facial expression and verbal behaviour; the second shows a lack of social skills (the passive people) and we tend to avoid situations that are a source of discomfort.

So a first step would be to identify our behaviour style and the possible discomfort that certain situations can create.

Identifying others' behaviour

We can discern behaviour style by close observation of the people we interact with. We have seen how learning to do this is essential in the section on assertive communication. When we are able to identify behaviour styles, we can begin to recognize the verbal and nonverbal behaviours of our interlocutor. We also remember that to execute this skill in a social situation we must not be feeling discomfort, so choose a low anxiety-inducing situation. Let's see some examples of verbal behaviour and try to identify behaviour style:

1. A friend arrives late to an appointment and we blurt out: 'I had to interrupt an important meeting to get here on time!'
2. A friend returns a CD we loaned him and on listening we realize it has been scratched and ruined. We say nothing.
3. We have an appointment, it is already late and our partner is still in the bathroom getting ready. We say: 'I sometimes think you do this on purpose, we are late and you are still in the shower'.
4. We are making manoeuvres to park the car when somebody 'steals' our place. We say to the driver 'Didn't you see me trying to get into that space?'
5. We are in a no-smoking area. Someone lights a cigarette; the smoke bothers us, but we say nothing and move to a different area.

It is easy to recognize the behaviour types in these examples. Aggressive behaviours are those numbers 1, 3 and 4, while passive behaviours are in 2 and 5. Now try to change each into assertive behaviour. I'm not going to write the answers here (I'm practicing assertive behaviour!).

Now that we can recognize our own and other people's behaviour, we must consider whether change is due. Remember the process should be slow and steady. But does change of behaviour mean simply modifying our verbal and non-verbal behaviour?

Are we really able to control our non-verbal or nonverbal behaviours without triggering emotional responses under verbal abuse or under provocation?

Look at the following sequence:

1. We feel provoked.
2. We meet the person causing our upset.
3. We activate negative emotional responses.
4. We know that we must be assertive.
5. We are tense when we issue the assertive behaviour.
6. What we say is formally assertive, but we haven't fully managed our tone of voice or facial expression.
7. Our words have no immediate effect on the person.
8. We are criticized.
9. We are no longer able to control our emotional responses.
10. We become aggressive or passive.

As we can see, behaviour has a before, during and after. In the above example, behaviour is observed during the interaction from the second through to the tenth consideration. So here we must examine the first. We believe we were provoked, therefore the other's behaviour was incorrect. This is a cognitive error, which can produce a sense of frustration or anger towards that person. But does feeling angry serve a purpose? No, it only makes us feel bad. If we feel bad, it is our own fault, therefore we need to modify ourselves. In the previous sequence we can identify the cognitive errors that do not allow for assertive behaviour. These are:

a. Others have to behave as we expect them to (Expectation).
b. We must never rise to provocation; our dignity is at stake (Pride).
c. Those who don't do as we expect can only be negatively judged (Judgement).

In this situation, if we want to issue assertive behaviour we must dismantle all negative thinking. So we neither feel pride or the need to judge, nor do we create expectations.

It is not easy, obviously, to rapidly modify our cognitive processes, but if we do decide to change, gradual practice will lead to us to identify our cognitive errors.

An analysis of suppositions

Learning from the past

As we begin to explore our past behaviour we can answer the following questions:

1) Were there some unachieved expectations that upset me?
2) Were there times when I expected someone to behave as I wanted?
3) Have I ever got angry for not accepting someone else's behaviour?
4) Have I got upset and blamed it on someone else?
5) Have I accepted any ambiguous behaviour (i.e. someone who behaves with us in one way but differently with others)?
6) After asking questions have I felt unsatisfied with the answers?
7) Have I created false expectations?
8) Have I been told that I gave wrong information or created false expectations?

9) Was I unable to refuse a request fear of offending?

10) Have I ever said: 'He's just saying that to keep me happy, I know he thinks differently'.

11) Have I given huge importance to someone or something, and not having been able to obtain it or having lost it, did I get upset?

We can identify two types of situation in our past, those in which:

1) We have upset others.
2) We have been upset.

We have to attach our supposition to the situation we consider most appropriate.

The correct suppositions inherent to expectation could be:

1) Do not expect others to behave as we want.
2) Others are not to be changed.
3) We should not be upset and if we are, it is only our own fault.
4) Do not create false expectations.
5) Everyone is under environmental pressure.
6) Do not ask questions if you do not know how to gracefully accept the answers.
7) Others have the right to make requests and we have the right to refuse.
8) Do not interpret.
9) Everything is important but not so much.

Now attach the situation to the new supposition:

Situation		Supposition
1	→	3-9
2	→	1-2
3	→	2
4	→	3-1
5	→	5
6	→	6
7	→	4
8	→	4
9	→	7
10	→	8
11	→	3-9

This of course is only a suggestion and you can identify more. Indeed, better to elaborate further suppositions; remember nothing is absolute.

Consider some previous circumstances:

1) Have I been upset about any negative criticism received?
2) Have I been upset in company of someone I considered important?
3) Have I made negative remarks about somebody?
4) Have I distorted the truth about myself to give a good impression?
5) Have I failed to reach a goal I set for myself and thought: 'I've got no willpower?'
6) Have I got angry with someone believing that if they had put in more effort they would have achieved better results?
7) Have I behaved inappropriately in a situation, for example, I was aggressive, but justified myself and blaming my behaviour as a response to someone else's behaviour?

8) Have I asked myself questions knowing I will not find adequate replies?

9) Have I denigrated someone's values to appear superior?

10) Have I believed it correct to judge what was right or wrong?

11) Have I negatively predicted my future performance?

12) Do I believe I am the most important person in my partner's life?

13) Was I hurt when a person I consider important in my life left me?

14) Did I feel resentment towards my former partner knowing they are satisfied with their new relationship?

15) Have I said: 'You are a selfish' when they didn't behave in the same way as I did?

16) Have I worried excessively for someone else's problem, despite knowing I cannot do anything to help?

17) Does it bother me seeing a friend's success (economic or sentimental)?

18) Have I ever felt that success often depends on luck, or on incorrect behaviour?

19) Have I ever borne a grudge and thought: 'He shouldn't have done that to me?'

20) Dissatisfied with a friend's behaviour have you ever said: 'I'd have never done that to you?'

21) Have you ever said or thought: 'After all the sacrifices I made for you, what I have I had in return?'

Now attach the corresponding suppositions to each situation. The various suppositions are divided into sectors, but such areas are purely formal as some suppositions may belong in more than one sector. We previously saw nine suppositions that could sit in the 'expectations' area, these however may also be used in the situations listed above. Let's look at the remaining ones:

Judgment

22) We can only judge our own behaviour.

23) Everyone is important, but not so much so.

24) We do not have the right to judge others.

25) We do not have to prove our worthiness to others.

Willpower

26) Do not attribute lack of willpower to self or others.

27) Do not justify your own behaviour.

Pride

28) Ask only questions to which we already have an answer.

29) Do not put others down to appear better.

Error

30) We do not have the right to say: 'I know what is good or bad for you'.

31) Do not make negative predictions.

Possession

32) We do not have the right to possess anyone.

33) We can only count on ourselves.

34) Possession equals being upset.

35) Be happy for other people's happiness.

Selfishness

36) Do not make other people's problems our own.

Envy

37) Who envies, does not change.

38) Who thinks for themselves does not have time to worry over other people's success.

39) Do not say 'I gave you...'.

It may be difficult to accept these and the ones we need to work harder on are the ones which will reduce discomfort. Remember that to reduce the discomfort we must face up to it. For example, if we are uncomfortable speaking in public, we can avoid the situation but for sure we will never reach our objective which is indeed, public speaking. We can make a choice only when are comfortable in any situation. Only if you no longer feel uncomfortable speaking in public can we really decide which behaviour to issue, that is whether to speak or not in public; here *we* decide - it is not the discomfort or anxiety that decides for us. You may think that accepting these suppositions may appear as a sort of non-involved, passive and detached living. On the other hand, you could think of it as starting point for getting involved in a more satisfactory, rewarding and happier life. How can we really spend a relaxed evening with friends if we are afraid of their judgment or we feel we have to constantly prove our worth?

How can we maintain the effort to reach our goals, if we only get upset by our unachieved and lofty expectations?

To the first question above and to *truly* enjoy an evening with friends, we must dismantle a few of our mistaken suppositions:

1) 'I have to show up as the best'.
2) 'I have to do what others expect so I can be accepted'.

To the second question, if we wish to continue making projects for our future and actively strive to reaching or goals, we must learn how to manage the frustration of failure. And to handle that we must attribute little relevance to all life's foibles. Putting too much importance on reaching goals is a source of huge frustration and we will stumble at our first attempt. It can be challenging to promptly respond and engage in new activities when discomfort endures in time.

If we believe that quality of life is a priority then we must learn how to be comfortable and thus gain pleasure from what we do.

Conclusion

How can we ensure that the suppositions we have rationally accepted become truly ours; that is, they become our new behaviour? Of course we rationally accept, for example, that is incorrect to presume others will behave as we want them to. The problem is that when we are in a situation where someone's behaviour is unwelcome, two things can happen:

1) We avoid them, because their behaviour is a source of discomfort.
2) We try to change their behaviour. Actually, on closer observation we see that in both cases we are focused on the other's behaviour, not on ours.

So it is impractical to think: 'Why do I have to change, when the other guy is doing the wrong thing?' or: 'Why, discomfort apart, do I have to modify my behaviour and therefore pay the price?'

Practice

If we have accepted the suppositions we must now turn them into manifest behaviour and, to achieve this you must:

1) Have memorized the suppositions that we are rationally capable of accepting.
2) Have identified the behaviours we want to change.
3) Begin changing only one or two behaviours at a time.
4) Focus on the behaviours to be changed.
5) Not expect short-term results.

When we have been repeating same behavioural sequence for many years, and we now want to change, you need to make a continuous and systematic effort. Rationally accepting suppositions is only a starting point for the work we must do. Remember you will only regress by convincing yourself:

'I'll never make it'.
'I can't change change my behaviour, this is how I am'.
'These suppositions are only pure theory, real life is different'.

If we decide to make a change it is fitting to practice in real situations. We have to phase out the old behaviour and start replacing it with the new. Let's see an example. We recognize how we become aggressive when 'under attack'. The behavioural sequence we want to change is therefore:

1) Your work is criticized in a manipulative way in front of others.
2) You are uncomfortable.

3) We think: 'Now I'll show them who is right' (we are getting
   aggressive).
4) We are verbally hostile with our aggressor.
5) We justify (to ourselves) our behaviour.

To reduce our aggressive behaviour we have to change step
3. Then, as soon as we recognize our discomfort or anger we
have to think: 'I don't need to prove my worth to anyone'. Also
we have to remember not to self-justify our behaviour. Only
once we have reduced the discomfort the situation created, will
we be able to provide assertive verbal behaviour.

Let's see a sequence which shows how we have a tendency to
interpret:

1) We invite someone to dinner.
2) We are courteously declined with the words: 'I don't enjoy
   going out in the evenings'.
3) We feel uncomfortable.
4) We think: 'If he/she doesn't want to come it's because they
   are not interested in me, I won't investigate further as I
   might put them in an embarrassing situation'.
5) We avoid calling again although we are interested in this
   person.

Here, our change process starts at step 4, that is, we do NOT
interpret the words said.

Let's see how we can use the internal dialogue to modify our
behaviour:

Once we are aware that we are heading towards a negative
emotional response, we must switch our thoughts to a more
suitable supposition that will help handle that emotion. Repetition is the key to change, we continually and repeatedly sub-

stitute the old thought with a new empowering one. Once we become aware that this thought is actually reducing our discomfort, because we have accepted it as true, can we say we have really changed.

Where there is discomfort, there is no choice.

We can follow the sequence:

1) Reduce discomfort by facing up to it.
2) Acquire new behaviour skills.
3) Decide which behaviour to execute, that is, make a choice between the behaviours we have mastered.

I fully believe that when we are able to make choices that are not guided by our own discomfort then we can consider ourselves free.

I thank my friend Joseph Wolpe for saying: 'Seeing how you like behaviour therapy, why don't you write down what you know to help others'. Thus giving me the incentive to write this book.

To Joannis Buras, Adriano Corao, Achille Delpiano, Aldo Galeazzi, Gianfranco Goldwurm, Fiorenzo Guglieminotti, Paolo Meazzini, Sergio Mottura, Fulvio Richetto, Roberto Sacco, Ely Schaftari, Piero Simondo, Silvano Zamuner. I have spent much time with all of you, often drinking until the wee small hours, and more often than not conversing about absolute trivia, I thank you all.

Special thanks to my friend Renato Tomba for helping me write the draft.

9 781985 849273